Skagerrak and Back:
Zophiel's Two Summer Cruises in 2007

Martin Edge

These scribblings are dedicated to my other half, Anna Pizzamiglio, without whose help this trip would have been halfway between unpleasant and impossible.

Skagerrak and Back
Zophiel's Two Summer Cruises in 2007

Martin Edge

First Print Edition 2014
Published in Great Britain 2011 by Martin Edge.
Copyright © Martin Edge 2011

The full sets of colour pictures from this and other volumes of Zophiel's travels are available free at:

http://www.edge.me.uk

Table of Contents

Page

Preface

Cruise 1   5

Cruise 2   6

Part 1 – Heading Norgewards   6

Part 2 – Gorgeous Norge   11

Part 3 – Solo Through Sweden   29

Part 4 – Doing Denmark   34

Part 5 – Amongst the Germen   40

Part 6 – Going Dutch   47

Part 7 – Beautiful Belgium (probably)   65

Part 8 – Vive La France   66

Part 9 – Drear Old Blighted   69

Part 10 – Home Sweet Home   74

Zophiel under the Forth Road Bridge in slightly better conditions

Preface

This is the holiday journal of a floating, ranting wimp. It is the tale of that wimp's progress round the seas of northern Europe.

In 2003 I bought a small and slightly scruffy yacht called *'Zophiel'*. Though rather small for long distance cruising, the cutter rigged Vancouver is a seaworthy heavyweight. The first one was designed for a couple of nutters who were emigrating from Canada to New Zealand and wanted to do it in a 27ft sailing boat. Other Vancouvers have crossed oceans and sailed round the world.

My ambitions are rather more modest. Actually that's not true. I'd love to join the ranks of the fearless ocean navigators and sail round the world. But, as I've already mentioned, I'm a bit of a wimp.

So over the past few years I've spent summers cruising around parts of northern Europe from Zophiel's base near Edinburgh. Most of these journeys have been sailed solo but sometimes I've had a crew, particularly for the longer sea crossings.

"Skagerrak and Back" is the tale of the first of these trips, in the summer of 2007. I wrote the account intending it to be a sort of extended log of the journey. My tendency to rant about everything I see around me has been, as usual, my downfall. So to distinguish between simple descriptions of the trip and observations about the landscape, wildlife, customs, economy, politics and boats of the places I visited, I have rendered the latter in *italics* and headed them *'Pondering'*. I hope you won't find this somewhat unusual schema too annoying.

By 2007 I'd spent four seasons exploring the coast of Scotland, north-east England and Northern Ireland aboard Zophiel. This had culminated in 2006 in a circumnavigation – more or less – of mainland Scotland. In 2007 I decided that the time had come to expand our horizons. The plan was to try for a North Sea Circuit. I would head to Norway then round the coast to Sweden, through the Skagerrak and Kattegat to the Kiel Canal, then through the Dutch inland waterways and back up the east coast of England. Normally, the short North Sea crossing, heading north-west on the return leg, would avoid heading into the teeth of the prevailing south-westerlies in September. But in the summer of 2007 concepts like 'prevailing', 'normal' and indeed 'summer' had little meaning.

The follow-up account to this volume is "Floating Low to Lofoten". This describes Zophiel's 2008 cruise along the coast of Norway to above the Arctic Circle. A third volume, "A Gigantic Whinge on the Celtic Fringe", is an account of Zoph's 2011 circumnavigation of Ireland and a fourth, "Bobbing to the Baltic" is an account of her voyage from Edinburgh to the Russian border with Finland in 2012.

Martin Edge, December 2011

Cruise 1

We set off from Port Edgar, under the Forth Bridge, heading for Peterhead – en-route to Norway - bright and early on June 16th at 6 am to get the full effect of the spring ebb out of the Forth. The crew for the first leg to Peterhead was two ~~victims~~ volunteers from Port Edgar Yacht Club - Ian Cameron and Jon Roberts - and me. We'd had a series of north-easterly gales of late, but the previous day's strong north-easterlies were predicted to die away, leaving gentle enough conditions for the trip. Just before we left there was certainly very little breeze in the marina.

The first major problem circumnavigating the North Sea was getting out under the Forth Rail Bridge. The wind was back up to 30 knots from the east and wind-over-tide created a steep sea that had us practically stopped. Half the crew – Jon Roberts – began to look a bit green round the gills.

We battered away in the hope that conditions would improve outside the main flow of the tide, but the wind and the steep sea kept increasing. This was quite surreal. I was expecting to have to face dodgy conditions at some time, but this was my home mill-pond. Between us we'd sailed under the bridges thousands of times. This was supposed to be the easy bit.

After about an hour and a half of motoring as hard as we could we'd covered just under four miles. We decided to stop amongst the moorings off the small Fife town of Aberdour for breakfast to see if the predicted lessening in the wind would happen. We picked up a vacant buoy. It was so rough on the mooring that Jon was too busy chucking up over the side to eat his vegetarian bacon buttie, which was probably a blessing. The other half of the crew, Ian Cameron, then announced that the heads was broken and indeed there seemed to be some blockage preventing it flushing.

Clearly the gods did not intend us to get to the Skagerrak. We gave up and sailed back under deep reefed main and staysail, surfing at 7 knots, which is fast for Zophiel, honest, arriving back on the pontoon at 9.30, about 3 months, a week and eight hours early.

Back at Port Edgar there was a mutiny as both the crew refused to countenance another 6 am departure the following day – especially without a functional bog. Captain Bligh at least got as far as the Pacific before the crew mutinied. I got four miles. I spent the rest of the day with a mounting sense of futility and a plunger trying to clear an almighty blockage in the bog by all means at my disposal. Ah the romance of the cruising life.

A week or so later I heard that Ian had sent an account of our fantastic summer cruise to Port Edgar Yacht Club's cruising email list, explaining in humiliating detail how we got to Aberdour and had to go home. Thanks Ian.

Cruise 2

Part 1 – Heading Norgewards

Undeterred, the following day, again at 6 am, I left Port Edgar with my other half Anna as crew at high tide and got the benefit of the spring ebb and a working toilet as we motored out on a flat calm Forth with about 2 knots of westerly wind. A dolphin helped celebrate our exit from the Forth with the last of the ebb at 11.15 am. The only thing that marred our day of sunbathing was the inevitable haar that descended after 6 pm, bringing with it a force 4 on the nose. However we entered Stonehaven harbour in the early evening and rafted up against a 45 ft aluminium Dutch yacht for the night.

That evening we encountered Zophiel's big sister, the Vancouver 34 *'New Chance'*, dried out against a wall in the inner harbour. I had run into her (not literally) three times the previous year in different places on the west coast. I reintroduced myself to the skipper, Alan Cawthorne. It was after ten p.m, but despite the fact that I'd woken him up and he was in his jim-jams he was nonetheless friendly and civil. He is now, according to best estimates, 86 and virtually blind. His wife Rhoda is 83 and does the navigation, since he can't see the charts. Every year they go on an extended cruise. This year it was to be all the way round mainland Britain and out to St Kilda. She was disappointed that the last time they went they hadn't gone ashore, so they were having another go. Given that most people their age would consider a short game of bowls a challenge and getting up the stairs a feat, this seems to me pretty amazing. This spirit of quiet adventure, carried out without fanfare, is one of the best things about sailing.

The following morning we motored out of Stonehaven in poor visibility and headed for Peterhead. We couldn't be bothered leaving early after the previous two days' efforts, so we knew we'd have about 3 hours of quite strong contrary tide in the afternoon. After a spot of motoring we later sailed slowly against the tide in perfect sunshine but not enough breeze to do more than about 3 knots. Peterhead may be fundamentally a dump and the marina almost literally in the shadow of a maximum security prison, but it seems to put on a good show whenever we enter the harbour and this time the sun shone

Zophiel's wind turbine and wind vane steering

obligingly on its white sand beach.

Given the north easterly gales which were once again forecast to plague the North Sea, we left Zophiel in Peterhead marina and returned to Edinburgh by bus rather than taking out the necessary second mortgage for train tickets.

I spent the next few days annoying anyone I could think of who might have some knowledge of weather and conditions in the North Sea by phoning them up and asking for advice. It did seem that there would be a break in the constant north easterly gales for a couple of days as, like Moses parting the Red Sea, the isobars on the weather maps opened up and left a predicted corridor of calm between Peterhead and Norway on June 21st and 22nd.

I kept telling Anna that all the top round the world racers need sophisticated shore-side teams to support them with logistics, weather information, transport etc. Though unconvinced, early on the 21st she gave a reinvigorated Ian Cameron, David Dougal and me a lift to Peterhead. Arriving ridiculously early we breakfasted and said goodbye to Anna. We refuelled on the fuel berth – paying the lad on the quay four metres above by means of the exact change in a Co-op plastic bag on the end of a bit of string – and motored out of the harbour. By the time I turned to wave goodbye to Anna the land had disappeared into the inevitable haar – and we weren't yet out of the harbour.

Members of the Red Minnows

Official Dolphin Display Team

The two most scary things about sailing are climbing the mast and using the VHF in earnest, so I came over all forceful and told Ian to call the Coastguard telling them our plans. His attempts to describe the boat were impressive – talking about the cutter rig, estimating the length, weight and draft etc. "No" said the Coastguard "what colour is she".

There's something disconcerting about a proper open sea with no wind on it at all when there's the residue of yesterday's strong conditions still lurking. The sea surges about gently rippling its muscles in a non-threatening but assertive sort of way. You know it can't last and are always expecting every zephyr to turn into a hurricane.

The new AIS system proved its worth straight away in the 200m visibility. Ships we never saw appeared on the computer screen, complete with all the details of their name, speed, destination, length, beam, draft etc. One tanker, travelling at 21 knots directly towards us, suddenly changed course by 15 degrees to pass round our stern. Is it possible that he actually saw us on its radar and changed course to avoid us? It was very reassuring to think that he had. I thought all these big ships were supposed to be crap at keeping watch. Of course the AIS wouldn't pick up fishing boats and other small craft under 300 tonnes which didn't choose to fit AIS. But my view – not seen as terribly reassuring by the rest of the crew – was that at least if a fishing boat sank us they would be small enough to notice that they'd done so and might deign to stop and pick up survivors.

Could this have been the tamest, most trouble free North Sea Crossing ever? For 24 hours we had 6 knots of true wind from the east, then for the next 20 hours we had 6 knots from the north. We motor-sailed across a sea with a 3 to 4 ft swell and changed tack round about the middle without changing course. The most disturbed and choppy sea was just off Peterhead. After the dry-mouthed start and the haar, the visibility slowly and steadily improved until – round about the middle - we could actually see stuff. In good visibility you'd never be out of sight of an oil rig, in the UK sector at least. Passing an entire tower-block city, lit up from hundreds of windows looming out of the fog on solo watch at night is an eerie experience.

We had a bit of excitement on the first evening as someone (David) sat on the tiller-pilot and pulled its cable off. At first I thought that the breeze was shifting, then that the oil rigs were circling us rapidly. Eventually we came to the conclusion that it was us who were circling. Since we were all crap at steering to a compass course with nothing to look at, this could have been a disaster, but David spent half an hour mucking about with a screwdriver and bits of insulation tape and managed to fix it.

There was further excitement as the minder ship to a cable laying vessel motored over and hailed us on channel 16, telling us not to pass round the stern of the cable layer. I rather smugly replied. The AIS had of course already told us exactly what it was doing, how close we could pass, how fast it was moving, how many cables it was laying etc. It was quite surreal on such a quiet sea to come across a construction team just getting on with their jobs more than 100 miles from the nearest land.

There was yet more excitement as the heads broke again after some arguably heavy-handed flushing. No bog for the rest of the trip and heavy reliance on the bucket.

On the second evening we had a brief period under full sail, but the wind soon died again. Alone on watch around 10 that night I had a full hour's worth of performance by the 50 strong official dolphin display team. The water was so clear that you could see them swimming under the boat from side to side before jumping clean out of the water. Some would flop back into the water sideways, flapping their tails apparently deliberately to make a noise. Sunset and 50 dolphins putting on an exuberant display all around the boat. Fantastic. All three of us got our own private dolphin display at some point on our respective watches and it was an amazing, privileged experience.

> **Pondering**...*The way the dolphins converged slowly on the boat in a line from a long distance, then swam with us, led me to suspect that they were using Zoph as a fishing aid. I've seen this behaviour several times. After twenty minutes or so they would all converge, leaving Zoph to pass on her way, whilst a crowd of gannets would appear, presumably for some of the dolphins' leftovers.*

...going through their paces

During our wimpy crossing we'd said it would be good if the wind increased near the Norwegian coast just enough to give the impression that we'd sailed all the way across. Obligingly, the breeze increased and went round to the north within sight of the fjords, allowing us to sail up them under full sail, waving manically at passers-by. At 1.30 pm on June 23rd we moored on a pontoon at Hjellestad marina, Bergen, just next to a seaplane. We'd crossed the North Sea in ridiculously easy fashion and were inordinately pleased with ourselves.

Anxious to let Aberdeen Coastguard know we had arrived, Ian tried calling the Bergen Coastguard on 16 and had an odd conversation which began with the manny denying being the coastguard at all and claiming to be a radio station. He was incredulous that we wanted to tell anyone we had arrived. He then confirmed it was him we had to call and, when asked if he would tell Aberdeen Coastguard, said "yeah, sure, right" like a teenager agreeing to tidy his bedroom. One felt, inescapably, that he was not really arsed one way or another if we had arrived or sank in the middle of the North Sea.

Cities in the middle of the North Sea

Arrival in Hjellestad

Pondering... Norwegians don't believe in fenders or, most of the time, warps. Your typical Norwegian motors his boat into his U shaped metal pontoon arrangement, in which one arm is a pontoon you can walk on and the other is just a metal strut. He lets the boat bang into the pontoon, makes a mobile phone call, packs his bags, musters the children and then - and only then - does he fling a couple of fenders over the side and tie a couple of lines to the boat. The fact is that most Norwegians are used to tideless waters so fantastically sheltered that you scarcely need lines. You can leave your boat somewhere in the sea, near a convenient rock, without tying it to anything, go back to work for a week and when you come back next weekend it'll still be more or less in the same place.

Hjellestad is about three miles from Bergen airport but in the middle of a popular recreational area full of walks and nature trails, so I took a long and scenic bike ride on my folding Brompton while Ian and David went to buy a ticket home. (I already had my e-ticket courtesy of our shore-side logistics team). I subsequently discovered that every square inch of Norway is a popular recreational area and that every single small town is a fantastically popular holiday resort. It seems that Norwegians all just swap towns each year for the month of July and become tourists in someone else's. After my spot of tourism I spent the rest of an exciting afternoon dismantling the bog and fixing it again.

The following day we all flew to Scotland, Me to Aberdeen and Ian and David to Edinburgh, once the nice man at the check-in had actually purchased tickets for them. David's dodgy credit card had been rejected the first time they tried to buy them online. Imagine just turning up at the check in desk in the UK and trying to buy a discounted economy ticket for a flight due to leave in an hour. All very efficient, these Scandians.

One of the locals in Skudeneshavn

Part 2 – Gorgeous Norge

Business in Scotland concluded, Anna and I flew back to Bergen on June 27th. We saw that Zoph was still on the pontoon and that all the lines were OK from the air as we flew over her at about 50 feet. Within half an hour of landing we were on the boat and half an hour later - having replaced the half a tank of diesel we had used motoring across the North Sea - we were under way. A wee breeze carried us along under full sail and full sun. It increased until we were doing hull speed in a force 5. It also started drizzling. The afternoon which began in full summer holiday mode ended with us tied to a pontoon in the village of Fitjar, next to the skips at the back of a roadside Spar supermarket, on a lee shore with a wet blatter of dreich bearing down on us. On the positive side, I managed to get the charcoal burning stove going so it was nice and toasty down below.

The following morning we left Fitjar in no wind under a cloudy sky. We motored a complex route down the intricate channels and inshore waters that run practically the whole length of Norway's coast. Most of the coast is perfectly protected by a complex string of islands and skerries, the Skaergaard. The scenery was fantastic – wee tree clad rocky islets, each with one or more wooden houses with boathouses and piers and pontoons. The scenery was extremely twee. In fact it was tweenery. (A word I invented that day and which I now offer the English language, free of charge).

> **Pondering...** *Of course we soon found out that everywhere in Norway is filled with these twee houses and cabins built right down to sea level. Every small cove has a house in it and every house has a boathouse, its own pontoon and at least one boat, usually five. Every fjord more than a mile long – and there are thousands of them – has more marina places than the whole of the east of Scotland and every person – bar none – over the age of one, has a boat with an engine in it, by law.*

We stopped for lunch in the small, massively twee and rather scruffy harbour of Mosterhavn. The cloud lifted, the wind increased and after lunch we had a great sail on a close reach in the sun down to Sletta, then outside the rim of protecting islands and on to Haugesund. We motored past Haugesund, down a narrow channel and only just squeezed under a very narrow bridge claiming to have 12 metres of air draft, to what was supposed, according to the rather poor e-book pilot, to be Haugesund sailing club in a place called Royksund. We wondered why there wasn't a single sailing boat there – only motorboats – but tied up to a pontoon, used the showers and paid the very modest fee in an envelope in an honesty box. Later we went for a walk and discovered

Haugesund Sailing Club about a mile away. Not at all where the pilot book said it was.

Pondering... We had begun to realise just how crap this pilot book actually was. It's an 'e-book' written by a couple of americans in the style of a blog about their holidays, which they then want 20 quid for. If it was a free - or at least cheap - blog I wouldn't mind, but it was at that time the only English language pilot for Norway, casually put together and riddled with mistakes.

Every year there's a race between Stavanger and Banff - or Macduff, in the Moray Firth. The direction of the races changes on alternate years and this year it started on July 1st and was from Skudeneshavn on Stavanger Fjord to Scotland. A number of the Scottish boats taking part were from our home port at Port Edgar. Wanting to get to Skudeneshavn and meet up with them, we left early next morning. By early I mean 10.15.

Some of the tweenery south of Fitjar

One of the million or so island bridges.
This one near Haugesund

Pondering... On the west of Scotland you always seem to have to leave at about 5 am to catch the tide and on holiday get up much earlier than you could be persuaded to for work. But the Scandians, with no tides to worry about and the sun setting around half past midnight, seem to be a fundamentally lazy bunch in the summer and 10.15 is a decidedly early start.

We had a nice gentle beat down the fjord in a south easterly force 3. It was a slightly fluky breeze but surprisingly not blowing straight up the fjord and allowing us to sail right up it on one tack for 12 miles or so. By the time we were out in the open sea and heading for the intricate channels around Kvitsoya island – recommended by Andy and Pam Grand Slam - the wind had increased to a force 5 and the sea was decidedly choppy. As we identified the narrow channel into the island and got the sail down another boat came out and unfurled its jib. It was Grand Slam. The first British boat we'd seen and one of the few we would see in Scandinavia outside Skudeneshavn. We tied up in the fantastically sheltered and twee harbour at Kvitsoya for an hour or so.

Pondering... Every kilometre or so right down the coast of Norway there seems to be a fantastically sheltered natural harbour which would give perfect shelter from every direction in a hurricane. I think it rather affects the Norwegian attitude to mooring. Any old bit of string tied to a twig will do and fenders are something of a luxury.

By the time we left Kvitsoya heading for Skudeneshavn the wind had died completely and by the time we arrived in the outer harbour, where all the Port Edgar boats and other entrants to the race had been berthed, it was absolutely pissing down. We rafted up outside the Ronautica 40 'Grand Slam' and the Jeanneau 49 'Erin' and got the charcoal stove going to dry out our sopping wet things. It pissed down all night. A somewhat inauspicious start to the race build up.

The next morning dawned reasonably fine and cleared quickly to become a scorcher with not a cloud in the sky. Which was just as well because it was June 30th which of course, as everyone knows, is a major festival. My birthday. This year was particularly significant since I turned 40.... Well, entered my very late 40s.... OK so I was 50. A lazy day with early beers. The crews of the boats from the Forth, Erin, Grand Slam, Mrs Chippy, Hei Matau and the others were in boozy holiday mood as well, but you could tell that behind it, for many of them, was the slight apprehension of the North Sea race. Anna and I felt quite guilty to be hangers on and not part of the race. Mrs Chippy's entry in the race was particularly intrepid. They were billed as the crew of three blokes with three arms and three legs. One guy was missing an arm, another a leg and the third had no arms or legs beneath the elbows or knees. Now that's a spirit of adventure.

Boats at the Skudeneshavn Festival

Erin, Grand Slam and Zophiel rafted up in Skudeneshavn

For breakfast we took Zoph into town and tied up temporarily in the centre amongst the festivalling traditional boats. Skudeneshavn was packed to the gunwales with boats. The outer harbour, where the race boats were, was quiet enough except for the wash of some passing boats, but the inner harbour was so crowded that that you could walk from one shore to the other across the boats. Being Norway, it was mostly motor boats with pissed and – judging by the size of the boats, rich – people on them. On land it was even more crowded as people wandered around. To exactly what purpose I'm not sure, because there didn't seem to be anything to do but buy lunch, but just sort of having a festival I suppose.

Being a mean bugger I had arranged a virtual birthday party. I invited everyone I know to the Skudeneshavn webcam, pointing down onto the mass of boats in the inner harbour. Just before the appointed time Anna and I took Zoph down the crowded channels into town and round the corner into the inner harbour crowded with old traditional boats. It was so still and crowded that we could have just stopped the boat and left her there all night without tying her up. She'd only have moved a few feet. At exactly 9 pm we opened a bottle of proper actual champagne and toasted... well, me, I'm afraid. We got some cheers from other boats and an actual trumpet fanfare down the PA system from the temporary stage set up for the festival. The latter, I suspect, may have been a coincidence. An hour or so later my phone rang. "Where are you?" Asked a friend who has the misfortune to live in Bolton. She had driven up for the party and was standing outside our locked and bolted house in Edinburgh, wondering where everyone was. I carefully explained to her the meaning of the word 'virtual' and suggested she read her emails more closely in future. Later we found out that at least a couple of people had bothered to watch us on the webcam waving into thin air like pillocks.

Back at the Erin/Grand Slam raft, Andy and Pam Grand Slam had actually got a card and a birthday cake for me. Complete with musical candles. Apparently these are an essential part of Grand Slam's normal inventory. Odd and possibly a bit kinky, but it was very nice of them and I was quite touched. Cake and champagne drunk from Erin's endless boxes of actual real glass champagne flutes completed a pretty damned good birthday.

The following morning the race management was busy telling the race crews that, whatever they had heard, there was definitely <u>not</u> going to be a gale in the North Sea. Adding that, should anyone hear anything about there maybe being a gale, it was their responsibility to decide whether to go. That's their arses covered then. They also predicted that there would be between two and four metres per second (four and eight knots) of wind for the start of the race.

We headed out to sea at around 1.30 to avoid getting in the way of the race preparations. We sailed west for an hour or so in a rising southerly breeze increasing from force two to force four or five quite quickly. Then we turned back to see the start of the race. Anna wouldn't let me sail close enough to get good pictures, but we saw them all coming out after the procession into town, then start the race, with some of the smaller boats seeming to hang back and Erin fastest out of the blocks and seeming to be off to a flying start. God knows how the trimaran Hei Matau, whose propeller had apparently fallen off whilst crossing to Norway, managed the procession through town. As they sailed off into what turned out to be rough and difficult conditions, we continued east on a fast fine reach in twenty knots of breeze under full sail.

At around 5.30 the wind died and we continued under motor to a pontoon belonging to the Stavanger Sailing Club at Langoya island (confusingly one of the thousand or so Langoya Islands in Norway). A lovely spot, again recommended by Andy and Pam Slam. There were a couple of other yachts but we had a whole pontoon to ourselves and a deserted island to explore. There was one building – a clubhouse of the Stavanger sailing club - with toilets, a lounge, kitchen, games room and framed photos of all the past commodores since the Vikings. There was a visitors' book and everything was completely open to use. We used the freezer to make a block of ice for our primitive 'fridge' which requires a big lump of ice every day or two, on account of the fact that it doesn't actually work.

> *Pondering... Getting ice is not a problem in Scotland, where every supermarket sells bags of it, but is virtually impossible in Scandinavia. The first shop assistant I asked whether they stocked ice said 'What would you want ice for, it'll only melt?' It didn't seem to strike her that, if it didn't melt, we'd only ever need to buy one bag. I managed to get a bag of ice from fish packers and fishmongers a couple of times, but never succeeded in buying any in a shop.*

Apparently Langoya island is a favourite holiday spot. Of course, as I've said elsewhere, every single place in Scandinavia is a popular holiday destination for Scandinavians. We were told it gets very busy when the Norwegians start their holidays about the second week in July. Pah! How busy could it be? After all there's only four million Norwegians and about the same number of islands. We were to find out in due course.

As we sipped our G&Ts on our deserted island pontoon, listening to the gale warnings on the BBC shipping forecast on long wave, we were glad not to be out in the middle of the North Sea with Mrs. Chippy and the rest.

The next day, with a south east force 8 forecast, we didn't want to do anything too ambitious, so we cruised, under motor and sometimes jib, around four or five of the anchorages recommended by team Grand Slam. The wind got up to just about a force 6 at times, but in these sheltered waters that scarcely mattered and later it died away completely. We saw a porpoise and thought this unremarkable after the dolphin display teams across the North Sea.

Your bog-standard mooring in Stavanger Fjord

> *Pondering... Actually that was one of only two porpoises we saw in Scandinavia. They were joined eventually by a solitary seal. The multitudinous Norwegian islands may make ours look a little paltry in terms of*

scenery and sheer number, but they can't do marine mammals – or indeed seabirds – like we can.

After an easy, lazy day and a failed attempt by me to sail onto a pontoon, we switched on the motor and tied up at another sheltered island anchorage, Rossoy. Again there were only a couple of other boats, but again toilet facilities, a lawn with places for barbeques, recycling bins etc.

The following day we thought we ought to do a bit more adventurous sightseeing, so motored in a flat calm the 15 miles or so to the mouth of the Lysefjord. This deep and narrow fjord, about 20 miles long, is a handy southern example of the 'proper' deep, mountainous fjords to be found further north. As we motored up the Fjord through water which, though hundreds of metres deep, was the colour you get round sandy coral reefs, the wind increased to around 30 knots apparent on the nose. Presumably it always funnels up or down the fjord in this way. A quick squint at 'Pulpit Rock' and a scan of the horizon to see if we could spot any of the loonies who, apparently, fling themselves off the 1000 foot high cliffs tied to glorified umbrellas in what's called 'base jumping' – and we sailed back down the fjord under jib. Apparently you don't get the full majesty etc unless you climb to the top. We'll have to take their word for it as we were buggered if we were going to climb 1000 foot high cliffs.

The Lysefjord

After a quick stop for bread and milk at a shop near the entrance to Lysefjord, we anchored for the night opposite the entrance to the fjord in Adnoyvagen, a perfectly sheltered and beautiful little anchorage about 100 yards across and surrounded by cabins and boathouses amongst the trees. We were the only boat at anchor. Unfortunately the heavens then opened as I went for a walk and got drenched, but otherwise it was a perfect day.

Pondering... *There are at least enough boathouses and cabins around the coast of Norway for every man, woman and child to own 3 each. Many of them are arranged so that Norwegians can actually have their boats in their living rooms with them, a design feature that Anna fervently hopes doesn't catch on in Scotland.*

A royal yacht trying to muscle in on our 12 gun salute

...and another perfect anchorage

The next day we headed for Stavanger in bright sunshine under motor with no wind. We were surprised to find the old harbour area in the town so empty of boats as we entered it. We were however gratified to see that half of Norway had turned out to meet us. Crowds thronged all the quay sides waving flags and cheering. Several majestic old 1930s motor 'yachts' – that is large ships - were decked out in bunting and, as we reached the middle of the harbour, the only boat out on the water, they gave us a 12 gun salute with cannon on the dock.

Then a police boat appeared and frantically gestured at us to bugger off. Apparently they weren't celebrating our arrival but the Queen's 70th birthday. I stopped doing the royal wave at the crowds. These royal birthdays follow me around. The previous year I kept bumping into our Queen in her chosen mode of transport for her 80th birthday tour, an old CalMac ferry.

Anyway, because the main harbour was shut, berthing space was at a premium, but we were lucky to be able to grab the last space in the quieter new harbour a few hundred yards away. All very swish and new, with credit card operated parking meters. Every time you went to the bog you had to insert your credit card and the machine would – you hope – bill you 50p, not £500. Berthing in the city centre in this swish new facility was ninety Norwegian Kroner ('Norks' for short), or about 8 quid. This was by far the most expensive one we'd come across so far as well. We spent the rest of a good day wandering around Stavanger - resisting the charms of the fabulous Canning Museum, to Anna's disappointment - and had no more major run-ins with royalty.

Pondering... Tying up your boat for the night in Scotland costs the same as about 6 pints of beer. In Norway it's about half a pint.

The following day looked like a good weather window to head out of the Stavanger Fjord and down the rather exposed bit of coast to the south, without the fringe of coastal islands which makes so much of the rest of the coast such an incredibly sheltered cruising ground.

We motored round to Tananger with the sky progressively clearing until it became a beautiful sunny day. With a north-west breeze of about 6 knots we got all sail up, which gave us a wee push to assist the motor and increased our speed to 6 knots without flogging the engine at all. A fine easy day making more than 50 miles on a flat calm sea.

When we arrived in Egersund we wandered about the outer harbour looking for fuel. In various places there were pumps labelled 'diesel' which, on closer inspection, turned out to be abandoned and apparently derelict. We went into the guest harbour and hailed a Norwegian boat on a pontoon. We motored up close, I stopped the boat and went forward to ask the skipper where we could get diesel. As he was telling me that the only way was to carry cans from the petrol station, it dawned on us that the guest harbour was positioned at the entrance to a small river which, with all the recent rain, was in something of a spate. A strong current in this part of the world being a rarity, we were surprised to find ourselves swept down on the other boat. Happily I was able to blame Anna, since she was theoretically on the helm. With some difficulty we fended off and escaped, though the folk on the other boat remained somewhat frosty all night as they inspected their self-steering gear, which Zoph had been trying to demolish.

We got on a pontoon in the slightly noisy and rotten-fish-smelling harbour, inevitably next to a big marquee in which a poor rock band was conducting a sound test.

> **Pondering...** *Every village in Scandinavia has a rock festival in July. This involves pitching a tent next to the marina, running sound checks all day, then several poor bands playing a loud gig to, on average, an audience of seven. We came across at least five of these non-events.*

The following morning it was bucketing down, but the wind forecast wasn't too bad so we pressed on, after managing to get fuel with the help of a bloke on a building site who had some way of getting access to the semi-derelict pumps. I think he was a scaffolder sheltering from the rain who paid for it with his own credit card and we reimbursed him with cash. Which is way beyond the call of duty for your average scaffolder.

We motored out in the pissing down rain in no wind, following a Swedish registered Hallberg-Rassy 34 called Elinor for most of the day. At one o'clock we put the main up to limit the rolling then, as we crept past Elinor, at about three in the afternoon, the wind suddenly increased to twenty to twenty five knots on the nose and the sea rapidly rose to a short five or six ft chop. We continued to motor into this rather unpleasant chop, actually getting a bit of sea water on us for the first time since Aberdour.

Of course the increase in wind coincided with us approaching the peninsula at the southern tip of Norway. The chart marked where we were going as extraordinarily dangerous waters. Anna read from the Rough Guide, which recommended a trip down the peninsula by road for those who wanted to stare out to sea and marvel at the power of the oceans as they remorselessly battered the coast. Elinor and another boat which had been following us chose this moment to change course and head for shelter to the west of the peninsula, leaving us feeling a bit vulnerable.

Wondering if we were doing the right thing we pressed on, but within an hour the breeze moderated and turned south then south west, giving us a push as we continued to motorsail. We motored into the guest harbour in Mandal and tried to come to terms with the fore and aft mooring to a buoy and a pontoon favoured in Norway. The harbour was getting pretty full as Mandal is, inevitably, a popular holiday spot.

Later I spoke to the skipper of a massive Hallberg-Rassy 48, who said they'd had too much wind from the east outside Mandal earlier, so we were probably pretty lucky and timed it right.

A local troll sunbathing on Ny Hellesund

Ny Hellesund
Zophiel's eccentric mooring technique on the right

Pondering... Passing the southernmost tip of Norway was a milestone since, including my trip helping to deliver the Moody 38 Equinox the previous year back from her Spitzbergen trip, I'd now sailed the whole coast, at least from 70° north. Is the coast of Norway a window on what Scotland would look like if the clearances had never happened? A lot of the coast, particularly further north, looks like bits of the west coast. Parts look decidedly like bits of the Outer Hebrides. In Scotland we are told that these rural backwaters, more than 57° north and 150 miles from a major city, are fundamentally unviable economically. Travelling the coast of Norway you confidently expect, when rounding the next headland and looking into the windswept loch, to see nothing but a few stones, all that remains of some abandoned steading buildings. Instead, right up to 70° north and in some of the most remote and hostile parts of Europe, you invariably get a perfect village or small town of white and red painted wooden houses, with a small working harbour and quite possibly a shipyard or other small industrial concern. Norway has deliberately used its oil money to support these rural communities and make them viable. What did we do with ours again?

Despite being a popular holiday spot Mandal is actually quite a nice wee town with a few riverside cafes and some winding streets away from the quayside. The nature of the boats – here and in Egersund – was rather different to elsewhere in Norway. Fewer wee motor boats and gin palaces and more sailing boats that looked capable of going places.

It was also the middle of a major monsoon season. The following day it continued to rain cats and dogs and moving seemed like a poor idea, so we stayed put. I managed to realise my dream, since Bergen, of a full cockpit tent – seemingly a must on a Scandinavian yacht. I spent most of the day fashioning one out of the only tarpaulin I could find in Mandal's shops and a series of hooks and bits of bungee cord. It was a roaring success in the sense that, in the middle of the night, when the wind rose, it rattled back and forth and created a roaring noise that kept half the marina awake. Oh well. Best get a proper one made this winter.

Anna was dubious about leaving the following morning, so we took a walk for a mile or so to Mandal's quarter mile stretch of sandy beach. Apparently this is Mandal's major draw. Reputedly Norway's best beach it is actually below 58 degrees north and, being at the latitude of the Moray Firth, pretty much counts as the sub-tropics in Norway. Anna was persuaded by the number of open boats crewed by five year olds going out of the harbour that Zoph could deal with the conditions, so at about 1 pm we left to head further east.

Pondering... Every Scandinavian child, by law, is issued with an outboard motor at the age of 4. They must do compulsory practice razzing round the bay for at least two hours every day. This keeps them out of their parents' hair and as long as they can still hear the annoying drone of the outboard disturbing everyone's peace they know the little darlings haven't drowned. There's no way your Scandian sprog would be see dead with a pair of oars.

Though a sunny day it was blowing quite hard as we picked our way carefully through the rocks and islands. There was more or less perfect shelter from the sea, which enabled the wee open boats to motor around, but enough wind to travel at up to 4 knots under bare poles and no engine. We did unroll the jib and zoomed along at six to seven knots, me pointing out the various canoes, coracles and toy boats crewed by tiny sprogs to assuage Anna's fear that an ocean going yacht couldn't cope with the wind. It's quite amazing how far you can travel along the coast in perfect shelter with a fetch of no more than a mile or so, and how many river boats and unseaworthy craft ply along more or less the whole coast of Norway.

After only three hours we dropped a stern anchor and tied the bows to a ring on a rock in the astonishingly sheltered anchorage of Ny Hellesund. There were two entrances about 10m wide at opposite ends of the round, 6m deep bay, about 200m across and otherwise completely surrounded by low cliffs and rocks. Apparently – and inevitably, the royal yacht had been in the previous night as part of Queenie's birthday bash. God knows how they got the huge ship through the gap. A wee crowd of motor boats nuzzled bows first into the rocks, side by side, each with a stern anchor out. This is the preferred Norwegian mooring technique.

Moored in Ny Hellesund with Edge's patented plank

Pondering... Many boats in Norway don't have an anchor in the bow at all, only a stern anchor paid out on a roller or windlass. Given the puniness of some of the anchors, some of which are just stainless steel mushrooms that look more like something from Ikea for squeezing orange juice than anchors, a lot of them must get pushed bows-on to the rocks. However with no tides and perfect anchorages with fetches of a hundred yards, parking is a much more casual affair than in Scotland. There are more perfect natural harbours along each and every mile of the million mile Norwegian coastline than there are in the whole of Britain.

There were more boats in this perfect anchorage than we'd seen previously. We put this down to it being famously popular at the time, but things were getting busier as the Norwegian holiday season began to get into full swing.

My lack of experience in Norwegian mooring techniques probably made us a laughing stock as I tried various, probably non-standard methods. After bunging out a stern anchor and tying the bow to a rock, I managed to tie us between two rings on two rocks at opposite sides of a small bay. I was inordinately pleased with myself for this manoeuvre, which held us on long lines in a way that a hurricane couldn't have shifted. We carry a plank for use with fenders on rough harbour walls and canal locks. I was even more pleased with myself for an arrangement whereby the plank was deployed as a sort of boarding bowsprit sticking out a metre or so. We used this eccentric set-up a few times for hopping over the bow. Scandian pulpits are all cut away to enable you to board from the bow. Zoph's is defiantly British and impossible to hop over without Edge's Patented Plank invention.

We left Ny Hellesund at 11 the next morning heading for Lillesand by way of the apparently famously beautiful (and popular) channels of the Blindliea. As the wind steadily increased we motored, then motorsailed, then sailed under full sail on a fine reach in a nice force 5, down a series of complex and often very narrow channels which took a lot of careful but rapid pilotage, at up to 7 knots. As we entered the particularly narrow channels of the Blindliea, part of which involved heading to windward, we dropped sail and went under motor.

The Blindliea – literally more or less blind alley – is a mis-named channel which is even more perfectly sheltered than most of the Skaergaard and leads right through to Lillesand. It is particularly pastoral and lovely, lined with twee chalets and boathouses and strewn with boats – mostly motor boats from small speedboats to major gin palaces – from end to end. It's a sort of cross between the Norfolk Broads, the Outer Hebrides and Switzerland, if you can imagine such a thing. Perfectly calm waterways with little villages, pastoral mountains and wee rocky islands. Lovely and a bit surreal.

Pondering... Long ago the Western Isles were not considered the isolated backwater they are now. Far from presenting a barrier, the sea lochs and passages between the islands were the highways which put places like Iona at the centre of a civilisation, not perched on the edge as it is today. In Norway they still use these sea highways for practically everything. On the west of Scotland, if you spot a ship on the horizon, you can check your Cal Mac timetable and confirm that it's the one and only ship in this part of the sea. In Norway you play dodgems with cruise liners, scuttling ro-ro ferries, long distance ferries, hydrofoils, tugs, coasters, oil rigs, working barges, commuters in speedboats and a whole host of traffic which still recognises that the best way to get about is by water.

We tied to a pontoon in packed Lillesand harbour in hot sun, next to the neds' party boat. Since everyone in Norway has a boat, hoodies and neds also have them, albeit scabby little ones only worth ten or fifteen thousand pounds. Our neds had settled in for a night of boozing and loud music aboard a last generation Norwegian double-ended motorboat. The worst thing was that the music – a sort of sub-Abba scandian dirge – was crap. Unsurprisingly, Lillesand is a popular holiday destination.

The following day brought a bit of sun and a force 4 from the west. We motored and sailed and motorsailed then motored on an intricate and complex route through more of the incredibly complex rocky channels that make up the

Skaergaard. As we approached Allesund the wind died and the dreich settled in. It drizzled for most of the afternoon.

We led a flotilla of yachts into Arendal. Looking astern there was an odd optical illusion. The furthest away boats appeared in front of the nearest boat. This turned out to be the Father Dougal effect. (It's not small, Dougal, it's a long way away). The boat which I thought at first was nearest was in fact a long way away but staggeringly huge. Unusually for a yacht it gave out a signal on the AIS. It was an extraordinarily large sloop. She was 58m long, with a 10m beam and 5.5m draft. We watched the tiny little helmsman on 'Kokomo' sat in the tennis court sized cockpit about as far above the water as the top of our mast. They got the dinghy out. This involved someone pressing a button and the entire transom hinging up in the air. Out of the transom walked about 10 tiny little people standing abreast and coming only halfway up the transom opening. I half expected to see a nuclear submarine and a rocket launching system belonging to a Bond villain. I suppose it's not entirely impossible that this was a normal sized yacht crewed by tiny little miniature people, but I don't think so.

Later we spoke to a few people who had seen this giant. Most of them insisted that it was from New Zealand. In fact it was British registered.

> ***Pondering...*** *No-one in Scandinavia recognises the red ensign. Since the UK is the only country in the world not to fly its normal national flag at sea, it is scarcely surprising that this causes some confusion. Obviously people just assume that you aren't from Britain because it's not a British flag. By far the most popular guess is that you are from New Zealand. I have to confess not to disabusing a couple of people of this idea. It's far more impressive to have come from the antipodes than just across the North Sea. I'm not a flag waver by inclination and only fly a national flag abroad and because I have to. The Norwegians and indeed all the Scandinavians are so flagmungous however that it almost began to rub off. Probably it's just ego and the desire to be a bit different but I began to value the ensign and the fact that we were flying something different from everyone else. I regretted not having a St Andrew's flag on board, since it was impossible to buy one here. I was sure that the further round the route we went the more British – that is predominantly English – yachts we would see. I began hatching a plan to fashion a StAn's flag from bits of old rag.*

Later the weather cleared and we entered the chocolate-box village of Linger in full sun. Again we were apparently stalking royalty as the Norgian Queen's ship had been there the day before. Linger is a massively twee village spread over 4 small islands and, with the help of a friendly yachtsman, we managed to squeeze Zoph into the last fore and aft mooring to a buoy and pontoon outside the Sailmaker pub, an engagingly scruffy establishment into which we were almost tempted for an £8 beer.

Lingering in Linger

The view from Skutevikkilen

Pondering... Invited aboard the Norwegian yacht of the bloke who helped us berth, we learned that the wee rural cottages with boathouses which covered the islands were now changing hands for large sums. A law that you have to live in a house if you buy it is apparently being avoided by the Oslo rich, who pay people a salary to live in their holiday homes for them all year. A few enquiries didn't yield any clues as to how to land a job as surrogate millionaire. It was obvious to us, coming from the UK, that these houses would be worth a fortune and sell as second homes. Yet the Norwegians described it as a new and surprising phenomenon. They seem to be catching our disease in which the only thing worth investing in is property.

Though perfect and perfectly friendly on the face of it, rowing about the four islands by dinghy it was difficult to find anywhere to land. The islands all seem to be fully privatised, with jetties and pontoons in front of every house liberally sprinkled with 'keep out' signs.

The next morning was perfectly sunny and perfectly calm as we headed west, mainsail up for stability only. We had a few recommendations for anchorages from a half Swedish half Indonesian family filling the tiny yacht on the next pontoon who we'd chatted to in Linger, as we headed out on another of the sections of coast that the Norwegians regard as extraordinarily dangerous on the grounds that it isn't perfectly sheltered by islands.

We got in a nice bit of sunbathing before we arrived at the apparently gorgeous island of Jomfruland, a long sandy spit very atypical for Norway. It's attractiveness seemed largely to be based on the fact that it was low and flat and unlike anything else in Norway. The Norgians must get sick of startling beauty and hanker after a dull bit of beach. They certainly liked it. The harbour was full to overflowing and boats were anchored everywhere.

Pondering... The minimum size of yacht allowed by Norwegian law is 40ft. The maximum age a yacht can be is 5 years, after which it must be destroyed or exported. It is allowable to have smaller boats as tenders, but these have to be towed at all times and must have steering wheels and at least 20 horsepower outboards.

We gave up the search for a viable mooring here and headed to another recommendation, the perfectly sheltered little bay of Skutevikkilen in the Kragero archipelago. This was an astonishingly good anchorage. A round hole a couple of hundred metres across, with water five metres deep all over, in the middle of a hilly, tree covered island. The almost land-locked bay had a difficult entrance, about five metres across, in which at least one yacht ran aground while we were there. It is hard to conceive of any wind conditions which you would even notice inside. As is their wont all the Norgian boats (and our Swedenesian pals) were huddled round the shore, bows in to rocks, leaving tons of space to anchor, which we did. A walk up the hill to marvel at the view in the sunshine, followed by a meal on board with local mussels from the rocks around the boat... and booze... rounded off a pretty well perfect day.

The next morning we left in bright sun under motor, first in behind the islands, then outside, staying just ahead of some gathering showers. From nothing the breeze slowly grew to a SW three or four and soon we raised the main and motorsailed, then got out both jibs and turned off the motor for a while. After a bit of drizzle it cleared and we had a good sail in bright sun. After 20 miles or so we arrived in Stavern. At first sight the harbour looked overcrowded with rafted up yachts. We entered and found a perfectly good fore and aft mooring empty. I made a right arse of picking it up. At first I suspected that we shouldn't be on this mooring as it was too readily available. However it soon transpired that everyone else was just there rafted up on a shopping trip for the day. By night time a lot of boats had left.

A Dutch neighbour on a 45ft Swan – very posh – waxed lyrical about Zoph and said that he'd read that the Vancouver 27 was 'the best little ship in the world'. Zoph would have turned quite pink with blushing had her topsides not been brown with shitty staining.

Naturally enough Stavern was a popular holiday spot. It was difficult to see why, but people certainly seemed to flock to the funfair and the inevitable crap pop concerts. There's nothing exactly wrong with it, but don't bother crossing the North Sea or anything just to go there.

The deserving charity at the end of the world

The following day we motored to
'World's End' (Verdens Ende), a few rocky
islets with a picnic place and a guest harbour
at the entrance to the Oslo Fjord. Again this
involved heading outside the islands and a bit
of tricky pilotage around the rocks. Quite wild
and potentially exposed by Norwegian
standards. They'd obviously only just finished

Tonsberg Harbour

building the harbour for tourists. Clearly there weren't enough fantastic marinas
and anchorages in Norway, there being only about one for every ten inhabitants.
I was slightly peeved to see that this one was built with EC aid money. Hmmm...
Given a choice between famine relief in the Sahel and providing the richest
country in the world, already with the largest concentration of marinas on the
planet, with another marina for yachties, which is the most deserving cause for
charity?

In a properly hot summer afternoon we wandered around, noticing that our
fore and aft berth had a rather jaggedy rock about 8 inches below Zoph's keel.
No wonder that berth had been spare. We banked on the lack of tide to avoid a
grounding. Round here you just forget about tides because they are so small, but
actually they do go up and down more than 8 inches!

Despite it being Friday 13th we didn't hit the bottom, so in the afternoon we
sailed off down one of the various routes into the Oslo Fjord. As most folk
motored, we had a nice sail in a force 3, managing to negotiate a tortuous course
through the hilly channels under sail. We needed the engine once to go to
windward under a bridge, but otherwise we were the only boat of the hundreds
returning to port to do the trip under sail.

*Pondering... We made a big deal in Scotland about the Skye Bridge. This one
piece of unremarkable civil engineering, linking a large and relatively populous
island to the mainland, caused a fuss which reverberates down the decades. Every
small island in Norway with a population of more than one, which is less than
couple of miles or so from the next island, has a bridge which would have the Skye
Bridge cowering in shame, could a bridge cower. Huge soaring structures rise from
the banks and span the chasms between the islands. There's scarcely ever any
question about whether you can sail under them. The Norwegians use their seaways
and channels between the islands and aren't about to block them with civil
engineering, so the bridges rise high above the rocky cliffs of the islands. The cost
must have been phenomenal, but at least they get something lasting from their oil
money.*

We sailed increasingly slowly downwind towards Tonsberg. Eventually we
gave up and motored the last three miles or so, but it had been a good sail
nevertheless. As luck would have it we managed to get a good finger pontoon

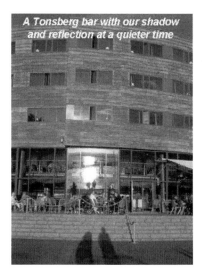
A Tonsberg bar with our shadow and reflection at a quieter time

mooring in Tonsberg guest harbour. We later found out that larger boats, including the Dutch Swan whose skipper was fond of Vancouvers, had to raft up on the town quay in front of the huge array of incredibly noisy pubs. This was the first example of many of the great advantage, in berthing terms, of being a relatively small yacht.

Tonsberg was as far as Anna was going. She'd booked a flight home while we were in Stavern. Being a Ryanair flight from 'Oslo', it left from an airport 100km from Oslo which, handily, was about five miles from Tonsberg.

Two and a half weeks from Bergen with Anna and we'd done 458 miles. Rather more than the distance from Edinburgh to Bergen, so not at all bad for gentle cruising. I was aware however that we were constantly and inexorably continuing to get further and further away from Port Ed, and would continue to do so for a while yet.

But Anna had another day yet – July 14th - and her birthday as it happened. To celebrate, it decided to piss down all day. Solid sheets of torrential rain which didn't let up for a minute. This suited Anna down to the ground, of course, because it meant she didn't have to listen to me grumping about how we weren't sailing anywhere. Her perfect day consisted of eggie soldiers for breakfast, wandering round the shops not buying anything in the morning and watching a DVD on the laptop in the afternoon. Nice and affordable. Anna had brought various nautical disaster films for some reason – things like ADRIFT! which consists of everyone falling off a yacht and drowning. Cheery. I was pleased she didn't choose that one to watch.

The only expensive bit was a restaurant meal and even that – an Indian – didn't hurt my pocket too much.

Pondering... Norwegians don't really believe in restaurants, only pubs. On the Mediterranean of course it's the other way round and basically every establishment is a restaurant of sorts. The British are the only people who insist on a strong demarcation line between the two. But a Norwegian restaurant – especially on a Saturday night, is basically a pub. People book a table, but then wander about boozing and finding somewhere for a smoke. Pretty soon they are all legless.

The harbour front at Tonsberg by midnight was a sight to behold, with the cream of Nordic youth paralytic in the packed 'restaurants' and bars, an equal number out on the streets boozing and the same number again sardined into motor boats and yachts rafted up 5 deep. Groups of lads would appear to hold conversations with half of them in the pub paying £12 a pint and the other half perched all over an old double-ended motorboat drinking the equivalent of cans of McEwan's Export. It seems the more expensive booze is, the more people drink.

I chummed Anna to Torp Airport the following day on the bus, then did odd jobs and stayed another night to catch the chandler when he opened on Monday morning. The reason for this was that I had caught a glimpse in his window of a fantastic exotic bargain. A toilet with the same fittings as my heads, reduced to half price! I duly purchased it and walked the mile or so back to the boat with it perched on my head. I was just about to cast off when I thought I'd just check that it was the right one. I opened the huge cardboard box to discover that, of course, it wasn't. I am now about half an inch shorter than I was. This is not an effect of post-50 ageing but the result of walking back and forth to the chandler a total of 3 miles with 2 different toilets perched on my head.

Part 3 – Solo Through Sweden

After the delay I was off and heading for Sweden in perfect summer sunshine and not a breath of wind. There was actually a marker buoy out in the middle of the sea like a border post and I was able to strike the Norgian and raise the Swedish courtesy flag with a suitable verbal fanfare. I spent most of the passage realising my ambition of having a Stan's flag by sewing one together out of bits of old tee shirt and sail mending tape.

After 37 miles I arrived at Koster Island and motored through a couple of village anchorages looking in vain for somewhere to moor. Of course Sweden is cheaper than Norway for booze and stuff, so attracts millions of Norwegian yachts as well as Swedish ones. It beggared belief that there could be any more Norwegian yachts given the number we saw in Norway, but there were hundreds on Koster. The Scandinavian dislike of simply anchoring meant that the fine sandy anchorage in 3m of water, away from the main villages and the fore and aft moorings on the two islands, had plenty of space.

Koster is a low sandy island which prides itself on having no cars. So all the locals, of course, ride about on really noisy motorbikes with holes punched in the exhaust pipes, which rather defeats the object. I had a very pleasant cycle about though. A sign for tourists in one village described it as being *"so quiet you'd never imagine it once was Sweden's second biggest lobster centre"*. I shut my eyes and tried to imagine the hurly burly of Sweden's second biggest lobster centre.

I motorsailed out the next morning at eight a.m. then had a good beat for an hour under full sail. There were few other boats about, due presumably to the lack of tidal imperatives discussed above.

The anchorage at Koster

Crossing the border

About an hour into the trip the black clouds gathered, the heavens opened and the sky was rent with forked lightning. The lessening gap between lightning and thunder showed that it was getting closer and closer and soon I could see where the lightning was hitting the sea. As I sailed along with my 12m metal mast the only likely looking conductor within 5 miles I tried to reassure myself that you never hear of anyone actually getting sunk by lightning. Do you?

After another hour or two the thunder storm passed and we were left with mere torrential rain. Battering against a force 5 down what amounts to the main channel up Sweden, by mid day there were more boats than I have ever seen under way before.

Pondering... Norway was a virtual boat free wilderness compared to this coast of Sweden. There was a constant procession of boats, mostly heading north, both motor and sail. There were a lot more sailing boats than in Norway and in Sweden it seemed to be legal to own a yacht of 30ft or so. Zoph began to feel less inadequate and puny.

I passed Fjallbacka, which was my fallback destination, and approached the entrance to the long and narrow Hambergersund. The chart showed a bridge over it with a clearance of 5m, yet a load of yachts were heading up this significant short cut. Others, however, were heading the long way round. My hailing of another boat to ask whether I could pass through caused some confusion, so I decided to risk it. In the event there turned out to be a new lifting bridge down this narrow, straight, canalised short cut, which was fine.

The Maritime Motorway down the coast of Sweden

A deceptively quiet bit of Smogen

Pondering... I found the PC based chart plotter really excellent, especially for the incredibly complex coastlines of Norway and Sweden, where I would otherwise have needed hundreds of brand new paper charts, instead of my scabby old second hand ones. The one real shortcoming with the C Map charts is their treatment of bridge height. In most cases they simply don't record it. Neither do they record whether it is a fixed or opening bridge. This can be rather frustrating. On a couple of occasions I decided that we couldn't be where I thought we were, because the chart showed a ruddy great bridge, which clearly wasn't there. Eventually I worked out that what looked like a bridge on the chart was actually, on the ground, a tunnel.

The CMap electronic charting has one further shortcoming. The Norwegian hydrographic organisation is evidently staffed by conscientious but pedantic and not very bright individuals. They have exhaustively surveyed every rock on the sea bed around Norway. On the chart plotter these appear as a myriad little black crosses. To find out how deep the rocks are you need to hover the cursor over each individual cross. The problem is that they record all rocks in the same way, no matter how deep. There is no way of distinguishing between a rock a hundred metres deep and a rock one metre deep. You laboriously hover over each one in the near certainty that you won't find one less than about fifty metres below the surface. Then suddenly you find one half a metre deep lurking in the midst, as the sea floor goes from being as deep as anything round Scotland to 'rock awash' in a few yards. Getting lazier as time passed, I probably missed spotting a load of these potential death traps, but happily the keel didn't find any either.

Arriving at the apparently popular holiday spot of Smogen I nabbed one of the last fore and aft moorings to a buoy and a pontoon available at the less popular marina near the bridge in the main channel. It was a bit windy and rolly with swell from passing boats but at least it was a viable mooring. I brompted into Smogen proper and my decision to moor in the less fashionable quarter was vindicated. Smogen was packed to the gunwales with yachts, rafted 5 deep for about a mile of harbour front. The westerly wind, which was now rising to gale force, whistled down through the boats creating a din of whining and clanking rigging. To make matters worse, Swedish youth in speedboats with go faster stripes and life threatening sound systems were competing with each other to make the loudest noise. To make matters worse still, the music they were playing was a sort of sub-Abba scando-pop. A pictureskew place to wander around but not a place to spend the night.

Overtaking a German Ketch in a force 7

A commuter suburb of Gothenberg

Back at the boat I was accosted by a Vancouver 27 freak. A local Swedish bloke who had been lusting after a Vanc for ages and was planning trips to Britain to find one. He knew all about them and was very complimentary. It was a nice change for me and Zoph after being slightly sneered at as the smallest boat everywhere. I invited him and his wee daughter on board to take a look at what was the only Vancouver 27 in the world with 2 toilets, albeit one was in a cardboard box filling half the saloon. He had cruised to Scotland years ago in a wee folkboat and wanted to do so again in a Vancouver, when he found the right one.

By the morning the gales hadn't subsided and weren't due to for a while. Most of this coast is pretty much protected by islands but there are points where windows open up to a long fetch to the SW. It was therefore with some trepidation that I headed off southwards into a SW force six to seven, gusting eight. Compared to the Piccadilly Circus the day before the sea was deserted, with only a few hardy souls out and about. With just the wee staysail and the motor for the bits which were too much to windward I made reasonable time, though in the exposed bits there was a heavy chop that was almost breaking at times. Not big waves – no more than eight feet – but steep and nearly breaking.

I headed inside Malmön Island and outside the exposed peninsula on which sits the town of Lysekil. This was a particularly exposed bit which then led into the very sheltered passage to Koljofjord and towards the east end of Orust island. It is here that all the famous Swedish yachts are made. Come here for your new Hallberg-Rassy or Najad or Malo.

Still under only staysail we were shifting at 6 knots with better than thirty knots of wind, but when passed by a nice old German wooden ketch (the crew of which gave me 3 cheers for having come all the way from Scotland) I changed the staysail for the jib and we caught the Germans up again. Round the east end of Orust the wind became fluky and after a few sailing attempts I gave up and resorted to motor. As we rounded Orust the GPS said it was 515 nautical miles as the crow flies to the pontoons at Port Edgar. I hoped that this was about the furthest away I'd get on this trip and that, in a sense, I was now on my way home.

Concerned that it was becoming increasingly difficult to find a berth I stopped at the first marina I came across on the south side of Orust and tied to the long main pontoon. We were the only boat to do so and a friendly Swedish chap off a small Hallberg-Rassy said that nobody ever really stopped here, but that it was fine to do so, and free. I always find it difficult to predict where will be hooching and where will be deserted, but this was a perfectly pleasant place to spend the night. A sort of suburban bit of the south east end of Orust island and the only place visited so far that's not, apparently, a popular holiday resort.

Pondering... Day 29 of the expedition and it my sad duty to report that a terrible disaster has struck. In the after part of the ship, in stern central beer store number 13,A,iv.45, upon routine inspection it was discovered that several of the beer cans had sprung leaks. No explanation for this disaster has been forthcoming despite a full and rigorous enquiry. Seven of our finest cans expired in this way and had to be consigned to a Scandinavian recycling facility, which was done with all due ceremony. They will be mourned by all on board. With 150 litres of beer, 20 litres of spirits and about the same amount of red wine on board, the bosun having taken stock, it was decided that the expedition, though much depleted, could continue.

The next day dawned cloudy but cleared to become increasingly sunny. I had a gentle breeze on the nose to start with which increased steadily as I beat under full sail towards Marstrand. As the breeze increased to a force five I tucked in one reef and put in a few short tacks round a headland. I passed Marstrand, then reduced to jib only for a fine reach south, following a long line of boats. I managed over seven knots over the bottom under jib alone in wind averaging 24 knots apparent and gusting 28 knots.

My fortunes seemed to have turned, at least temporarily, as the marina on Halso Island also had loads of free space in U-shaped pontoon mooring boxes. I had a pleasant wander by Brompton over this wee suburban island, providing accommodation for the posher part of Gothenburg's Volvo workforce. I fell into conversation with a family whose sprogs were interested in the Brompton. Talking to the parents proved difficult since the 5 year old sprog was outraged that I – and his parents - were apparently talking complete gibberish. Though nothing new, in this case it was just the fact that I was talking English that disturbed him since the concept of a foreign language was new to him. "WHY ARE YOU TALKING LIKE THAT? STOP IT? WHY ARE YOU TALKING RUBBISH?" He demanded repeatedly in Swedish, according to his parents.

The next day was earmarked for a long passage, so though I'd have liked a favourable breeze I was grateful enough for the full sun and force 0 that greeted me in the morning. I had a very pleasant but uneventful motor the 65 miles to Anholt Island. Uneventful aside from dodging the thousands of ships spewing out of the Baltic up the main shipping lane, that is. There was another ceremonial verbal fanfare as I struck the Swedish flag and raised the Danish. Anholt is noticeably Danish, being a big lump of sand washed up in the middle of the Kattegat. But it is surprisingly high, steep and striking, for a lump of sand.

Approaching Anholt with its forest of masts

Part 4 – Doing Denmark

The first thing that struck me about Anholt from a distance of about 10 miles was a glistening, shimmering patch of vertical stripes on the horizon. As I got closer this resolved itself into about half a million masts in the harbour. Boats had filled the fore and aft mooring spaces. More boats had come and wedged themselves in the small gaps between the spaces. More boats had then put out stern anchors and nudged their bows between the sterns of all these boats. Then more boats had come along and moored cross-ways along the sterns of these boats. Then a load more boats had come along and rafted up about 8 deep along these boats. Being wee, Zoph can usually find a space and people on larger boats are often grateful to get a small boat outside them since it might deter other, larger boats.

I rafted up alongside a deep slab of boats, against a scruffy looking big Jeanneau crewed by a fantastically pissed Dane and his only slightly more sober cockney mate. They looked like superannuated heavy metal roadies – and may well have been for all I know. I was invited on board for a beer and became slightly embroiled in the argument they had with the harbour staff as they refused to pay the mooring fee, which was the highest I'd seen so far in Scandinavia at nearly half what you'd be charged in Port Edgar and a quarter of the southern English going rate! Exorbitant.

In the morning I took a Brompt trip round half the island, with its camping hippy youth denizens. Anholt has quite a nice laid-back atmosphere with very few cars, which I suspect is quite a good thing due to the chemically altered concentration levels of some of the inhabitants.

The main reason for crossing from Sweden this far north, as opposed to tracking further down the Swedish coast first, was that you are absolutely guaranteed westerlies in summer in this part of the world. Since Denmark was a weather shore whilst Sweden was a lee shore it made sense to cross to Denmark. Easterlies, I was reliably informed, are virtually unheard of in the summer months.

At about 11 am I headed off confidently under full sail reaching towards the mainland in a south easterly force five. Soon I put a reef in the main, then another and we surfed along in a steady 25 knots apparent south easterly wind with the breeze abaft the beam, gusting to over 30 knots. With probably about 35 knots true south easterly wind we peaked at 9.1 knots over the ground (against a theoretical current which the chartplotter identified), an all time world speed record (Zophiel division). Impressed though I was by the speed, I grew worried by the fact that the place I was heading – Grena – is a yacht harbour cut into a long surf beach, with a 3m deep entry on a lee shore with a force 7 to 8 throwing up breaking 8ft high steep waves. Would I even get into Grena, or should I head further south to Ebeltoft, or for the slightly deeper Grena commercial harbour, where there was a chance that the waves weren't breaking?

In the event a couple of hours later, as the sky cleared, the wind abated and I ended up motorsailing, then sailing under full sail in a gentle force 3, into the packed Grena yacht harbour – unsurprisingly, but unaccountably, a popular holiday spot – where I rafted up onto a large German yacht. Its skipper confirmed that, a few hours earlier, entry to the harbour would have been pretty difficult, with breaking waves in the approach. Though there was no actual space left to raft side by side, I managed to raft on at a sort of jaunty angle. It proved possible to rig the plank over the stern so that it just reached the pontoon past the German's bow. I was inordinately and childishly pleased with this new use for the versatile old plank.

Anholt sunset

...and another

I was awoken in the morgen at seven a.m. – fantastically early by Scandinavian standards - by the Germans next door, anxious to head off before the predicted northerlies started. As they headed north I headed south under motor, with the jib set to cut down the rolling in the left-over swell from the previous day. It was an uneventful motor to Ebertoft, made more interesting by the berthing in the marina. This was my first encounter with Baltic mooring boxes, which typically have a couple of wooden piles between which you motor, hanging a rope from each to the stern quarters as you pass, then leaping ashore onto the bow pontoon before you bash into it. A not entirely straightforward move single-handed, but there's often a Scandian or two hanging about to volunteer to take your lines.

In Ebertoft there was one space left, hard up against the side in a corner of the marina and empty because it was designed for a canoe. As I approached Zoph ground to a halt, her keel stuck in the mud. The harbour master waved me on. There is a bit of tide so I asked him whether it was high or low tide – springs or neaps. He looked at me as if I was insane, shrugged his shoulders, then suggested that, since there was a bit of seaweed poking out above the tide line, it might be low tide. Given this fantastic reassurance I put the engine into gear and slowly glooped along through the mud until she was more or less in the

mooring box, confidently expecting to be
'neaped' and unable to get out for a month
or two.

Anholt fishing boat

> *Pondering... This was a pattern
> repeated throughout Denmark, Germany
> and the Netherlands. As boats have got
> bigger – and in particular beamier – the
> fixed infrastructure of pontoons and piles
> hasn't been able to keep up. So narrow box
> moorings, ideal for a yacht like Zoph with
> her 8'8" beam, lie empty while the marina
> caravans circle looking for larger berths. It is not uncommon to see a big Beneteau or
> Bavaria ramming the piles to try and force a way in. I didn't come across many
> where draft was a problem, but if you're heading this way yourself, do so in a thin
> boat.*

Ebertoft is apparently fantastically lovely, but since it started pissing down
immediately after I'd moored up, and didn't stop all day, its delights were
somewhat lost on me. I did take a soggy wander around town and it was quite
twee in an obvious sort of way, but the weather didn't put one in the mood for
exploring jewels of Danish small town architecture.

Instead I employed myself gainfully by fitting the toilet, whose cardboard
box had been filling half the cabin through two countries. This turned out to be
surprisingly painless and in double quick time I had the pleasure of a smooth,
squirt-free flush. Somehow I managed to get the old one and all the packaging
in the waste bins by jumping up and down on them. Unfortunately however, in
the process I managed to knacker the ship's umbrella, making my subsequent
trip into town for a celebratory meal a somewhat bedraggled one.

> *Pondering... Typically, your Scandinavian village or small town seems to
> contain a whole pile of houses, a series of shops, some offices and a factory or two of
> some kind. This last might be a small shipbuilding yard, an oil service yard, a
> sawmill, whatever. The offices, even in quite out of the way places, might be the head
> offices of an oil service company. There is a sense that these settlements are whole,
> viable communities. This seemed to be the case particularly in Norway, but to a
> lesser extent applies all over northern Europe. Contrast this with similar towns in
> Britain. Here the residential area will be entirely separate from the shopping centre
> and in a completely different place from the industry. Indeed it is highly unlikely
> that there would be any industry in a small town, but wherever it was it would all
> be cordoned off in a nightmare environment behind a huge unscaleable fence, miles
> from civilisation. Even if the industry had closed down it would remain a wasteland
> closed off beyond the security fence. Perhaps our post-war planning system, with its*

obsessive zoning, has a lot to answer for. Perhaps we all suffer from nimbyism. But perhaps we should take a look at how the Scandinavians do things.

It seemed to be the rule this Scandinavian summer that if you sit through a day of pissing down rain you are rewarded with a day (but only one) of bright sun, so it was in a north-west four or five in bright sunshine that I headed off for the town of Juelsminde – billed of course as a paradise for holiday-makers – under full sail at up to 6.3 knots. There were a lot more boats out than the previous couple of days and for a couple of hours I raced a blue Sadler 26, and won. Of course they might not have known that they were racing and if I hadn't of won I wouldn't have been racing either, but I won!

Ebeltoft

A Dutch roadhog heading for Middelfart. I know it doesn't look like 40 knot winds, but honest it was

As I hardened up round Tuno island the wind obligingly went down to a force 3, still giving us a comfortable sail. However as it continued to go down the engine went on at one p.m. Under fluky wind conditions the jibs went up and down a couple of times before I gave up and motored the rest of the way to the popular holiday destination of Juelsminde, where once again we rafted up in a packed marina, this time onto a large Danish Beneteau, whose owner claimed it was a copy of a Swan. Yeah, right!

The law about alternating weather days still pertained, so the next morning it was miserable and blowy. It started with the surreal experience of being interviewed on the phone at 8.30 am for a job in the University of Sydney. It's quite difficult to concentrate on policy for architectural education whilst stood in your Y-fronts listening to the wind shrieking in the rigging and wondering about the day's passage.

My Danish neighbour, a ship's captain by trade, had assured me that we were due light and variable winds today, despite the force 7 forecast I'd been told about by my shoreside logistics team in Edinburgh. I wondered if he had superior local knowledge. He didn't.

I battered off, motoring to windward into a short five foot chop and an easterly force five. After a mile or so I was able to bear away and I got the jib out as I eventually went onto a broad reach. The wind increased to 20 to 25 knots apparent, with seven knots boat speed away from it. At its peak, surfing down 2.5m waves, Zoph was going 9.5 knots, again against a theoretical current, whilst the anemometer showed 30 knots behind us. But not to worry, 40 knot easterlies in the summer are completely unheard of round here. There was little other traffic about, though I was 'cut up' by an old Dutch tall ship, overtaking but forcing me to change course as she drifted across us.

Tall ships in Middelfart

Sonderberg

The sail would have been more positively exhilarating had it not been pissing down most of the time. As I turned into the narrows past the exotically named town of Middelfart the sea subsided and the wind dropped. I passed the tall ship again and motored down the channel round to the back of Middelfart, taking a box mooring in a pleasant enough marina with – halleluiah – loads of spare spaces.

Later I Brompted over to Middelfart harbour, where there were about 30 tall ships and a great throng of folk enjoying yet another Scandian festival, as usual involving nothing more than some beer and wandering around a harbour looking at things for a while. I also saw the first British boat for quite some time. A 45 footer crewed by about 9 specimens of posh English youth doing a circuit round Copenhagen and quite pleased with themselves. They'd stayed put in Middelfart today since they'd seen gales forecast. Middelfart. What a great name. I'm just enjoying writing it. Middelfart Middelfart Middelfart Middelfart Middelfart.

The next day I had a very different sort of force 6, the wind having shifted from east round to north west and the sun having broken through. A fantastic fast reach under full sail with a bit of favourable current saw us do 14 miles in the first 2 hours. This may not sound spectacular but it's pretty good for Zoph. Around us deep reefed 40ft Bavarias were

The bridge at Sonderberg

broaching all over the place as we tracked right through them with hardly any need to touch the rudder. Zoph knew the way. Most other boats were deep reefed from the start but Zoph held full sail well. Around mid day however I put 2 reefs in the main to beat across choppy open water.

A winding course saw us back on a reach, then a run, then hardened up onto a beat to pass down the narrow fjord towards Sonderberg. A short wait for the bascule bridge over the harbour to open and I rafted up on the town quay outside a Danish boat. A 6.5 hour passage with barely half an hour with the motor on. A cruising rarity.

Astonishingly, nobody on board my Danish neighbour spoke any English. The first monoglots I'd met in Scandinavia. It reminded me how lazy I'd got in assuming that everyone was going to speak my language. A quick Brompt around the pictureskew town of Sonderberg. Which is a popular holiday spot, apparently.

The next day brought more good sailing conditions and a fine reach in a southwest 4 or 5 under full sail. This was only marred by the fact that I was steadily overhauled by a small yacht that looked a bit like a folkboat and which, presumably, I should have been able to beat! Whatever I did however they kept catching me all the way. Zoph continued on through the water at the speed of a greyhound and, if you've ever seen a greyhound swimming, you'll know that's pretty slow.

There were all sorts of yellow buoys marking patches of sea which were probably military exclusion zones and so forth. My information was patchy on them. So we changed course to harden up and pass outside these areas and gain sea room for a reach to Kiel, as the wind was predicted to increase later.

Racing a Dutch tall ship

Part 5 – Amongst the Germen

Another verbal fanfare saw the Danish flag struck and the German raised. The German flag was the first one I'd used which is different if hung upside down, so I had to take care. It was gratifying under full sail to overtake a huge Dutch tall ship, but perhaps he didn't know it was a race. In the event the wind died rather than increasing as predicted and I motorsailed towards Kiel. Having been told that the Germans are sticklers for such things I rooted out a motoring cone which I remembered being on board when I bought the boat and which I hadn't seen since. It was only after a few other boats passed that I realised that, whilst the flag was the right way up, the cone wasn't.

I found a berth easily in the half empty marina nearest to the entrance to the Kiel Canal, reasoning that it would be easy from here to cycle to the entrance and check it out. On the chart it was clear that the canal entrance was no more than a few hundred yards away. Indeed I could clearly see it from Zoph's berth. I eschewed the British army sailing club next to the Marina, which British boats apparently flock to, as being way too jingoistic.

I then cycled in the rain to the canal. This took me an hour and a half, during which time I covered an estimated 12 miles, much of it up and down hundreds of dead end roads. The bloody British army has cordoned off a bit of the coastline. A perfectly nice little coastal suburban road covering the few hundred yards from the marina to the canal had been permanently blocked by twenty foot razor wire fences to protect the western world from my dastardly plan of cycling a folding bicycle along the seafront. Presumably this allows everyone to sleep soundly in their beds at night.

When I finally arrived at the canal basin I found that it was also surrounded by security fencing and the security guard couldn't enlighten me as to the procedure for passing through the canal. At least I did eventually find a shop to buy bread and milk and Eureka! bags of ice for the festering fridge!

Pondering... Britain and Germany are the only two countries in northern Europe where you can buy bags of ice. In these countries every tiny supermarket in every small town has a stock of ice. Everywhere else they look at you like you are insane if you ask for ice. Typically they offer you proprietary plastic devices in which you can make ice, if you have a freezer. The irony of this seems lost on your Scandinavian shop assistant. Since countries like Denmark and Holland are packed to the rafters with Germen, this seems an odd omission.

In the Kiel canal

The next morning I circled around under motor for a couple of hours in 30 knots of wind, pissing down rain and amongst an increasingly large and motley assortment of craft, waiting for the lock gates to open and let me into the canal. I finally heard an announcement that they wouldn't open for another two hours so, with some difficulty, I moored against the wooden piled dockside, against my trusty B&Q plank. No sooner had I done so, of course, but the lock gates opened and the milling throng headed into the lock. Closely followed by Zoph.

As part of the thrilling mong I rafted up against a Beneteau caravan with an unusually shirty and shouty crew – the first overtly unfriendly people I'd met since leaving Port Edgar – and waited for someone to come and collect the fee for transiting the canal. I was a little nervous about this, since I'd heard that the Germans were somewhat officious about requiring the correct documentation. It seems quite likely that this is just a bit of racial stereotyping, since in common with everywhere else I went this summer, nobody appeared to ask for any paperwork. I couldn't even work out what I was supposed to do to pay the transit fee. I think I may have been supposed to go ashore whilst in the lock and find an office. However the Beneteau bunch were already shouting at me for my fendering and it would have been impossible to leave Zoph unattended. Once I left the lock there was nowhere to moor. So in the end, though I did try, I paid not a penny for the almost 3 weeks Zoph spent in the Nord Ostsee Kanal.

I motored into a force 8 the 20 miles or so along the canal to Rendsburg. Every now and then a large ship, or a small convoy of large ships, hove into view. The ones heading east soon passed, but with an 8 knot speed limit the ones heading west seemed to take an age to pass. This was something of a problem single-handed on Zoph, with her utterly crap Flintstones electric autopilot. This tiller pilot had a small dial with N E S and W on it, which you turned to roughly the direction you wanted to go. Equipped with the sort of compass you might find in the sole of an eight year old's shoe, it's reasonably useful if you know roughly what continent you are aiming at, but beyond that aren't too bothered where you end up. It's utterly useless for heading in a straight line down a canal and I sat at the tiller getting drenched and gasping for a cup of coffee, as everyone else went past in their bloody pilot houses or under their bastard full cockpit tents, with their **** autopilots smoothly guiding them down the canal.

Pondering… By this time I had completely given up on my mid price-range Gill 'offshore' waterproofs. It may be that the top of the range breathable waterproofs manage to achieve the dual objectives of feeling like a nice soft bit of cloth and actually being waterproof. Your mid-range, £200 waterproofs, on the other hand, achieve the touchy-feeliness of a nice piece of cloth by the simple expedient of not bothering, at all, with being waterproof. After a few goes at wearing completely waterlogged 'waterproofs' I had taken to wearing the shiny plastic mac and trousers I got from Millets a decade or so ago for a tenner, which have never let in a drop of water. If you are a boatless member of a summer Sunday racing crew and it's not actually raining, wear wrap-around shades and red 'breathable' waterproofs. You will look cool, which is the main thing. Otherwise wear a warm jumper and a plastic mac. You will stay warm and dry, which is the main thing.

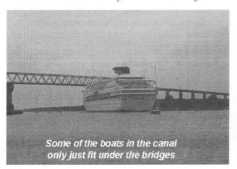

Some of the boats in the canal only just fit under the bridges

A bridge on the Kiel Canal. Passengers shuttle back and forth in the suspended car

I decided to call it a day at Rendsburg, which has the only real marina inside the canal and was rumoured to be the only place I could leave Zoph for a fortnight. Rendsberg is a nice old town with a marina crammed with half million pound plus yachts, with fantastic facilities, a restaurant and lounge. Despite the large demand, the obvious amount of money about and the facilities being about a hundred times better than Port Edgar, the weekly rate for Zoph was 48€ - which at the time was about 30 quid. There really is nowhere in the rest of northern Europe as expensive to keep a boat as the very cheapest place in Britain.

My shoreside logistics team arranged a flight home for me from Dortmund and I had to wait in Rendsburg for a couple of nights for the nice cheap flight. Predictably, of course, in the meantime there was a pop festival 20 yards from the marina. After the building of an elaborate stage and sound checks by about 10 bands all day, 23 people showed up for the actual festival at the weekend. A recurrent pattern. I wonder when it will strike the good people of Europe that there may be an over supply of summer festivals for yoof?

Rendsberg

Pondering... I chatted to one of my neighbours in Rendsberg, an Englishman with a 45ft Princess powerboat. He told me that, a couple of years before, he'd done roughly the same North Sea circuit as me, except he'd crossed to Bergen from Shetland because of his boat's limited range. He told me how much fuel the beast used. I calculated that, at European prices, it would have cost him about £13,000 in diesel alone to do this trip.

After a couple of weeks back at work I flew back to Hamburg. Except it was Ryan Air, so it flew to the Hamburg Airport that's about 200 miles from Hamburg. Cheap enough though and with a bit of luck the next time I needed to go home it would be by local train.

I'd been looking for a weather window for getting out of the Elbe – a nasty bit of shallow estuary with 4 knot tides against the prevailing winds in a corner of German Bight. It's quite well known as a spot to get trapped in for weeks at a time. The forecast didn't look too great as I motored the 36 miles down the rest of the canal to Bruntsbuttel into the showers.

Pondering... Everywhere, of course, is a popular holiday spot and in the case of the canal it was a magnet for thousands of camper vans. These lined its banks parked up for the day to look at passing ships, on one of the many camp sites lining the sides of the canal or queuing up for the many identical little ro-ro ferries which scoot continuously back and forth across it, waiting patiently for a passing yacht to aim at.

I found the last available bit of spare pontoon in Bruntsbuttel. About 28ft long and too short for any boat except Zoph. I was quite smug about my judgement and berthing ability.

The next morning I locked out of the Kiel canal – still without having paid my dues – with a force 5 to 6 westerly forecast against a spring ebb. Though the shallow estuary of the Elbe, with it's strong currents, does have a bad reputation, I put a lot of my nervousness at this down to having become canal-bound. Spend enough time in calm bits of fresh water and the prospect of the wide open sea begins to get more alarming.

I beat half of the way to Cuxhaven then, as I headed more to the west and into the wind, motorsailed the rest. In the event it was choppy and splashy, with short six foot waves, but no more than just a little uncomfortable. After making a right arse of berthing in the large marina I amused myself by watching other yachts making the same mistake as me trying to get into the harbour. First they'd point

On a pontoon in Bruntsbuttel

down river towards the marina entrance. Then they'd adjust their course continuously towards it until they were swept right past and heading – at 1.5 knots over the bottom – back the way they had come against the four foot tide. Cuxhaven, though an unremarkable town, was of course a popular holiday spot.

Pondering... German seaside resorts are like being transported back to the 1920s. Thousands of bizarre wicker sort-of-huts litter the dunes and the seafront at Cuxhaven. These constructions, when unlocked, turn into huge wicker deckchairs topped by sunshades, with lockers for keeping your bucket and spade and thermos flask. The pristine old chair/huts and the number of people wandering the beach and in the amusement arcade make it clear that, unlike ours, German seaside resorts are still the place to be on your summer hols.

A friendly Dutch chap on the boat next to me gave me a handy map of the Dutch inland waterways. He and practically everyone else seemed to be leaving at about 4.30 the following morning, to catch the ebb tide and a rare forecast of bugger all wind. Everyone was aware of the possibility of getting stuck in the Elbe and anxious to avoid it.

Kites at Cuxhaven

So at 4.30 the next morning we cast off and headed out into the darkness. This was a bit of a shock to the system after the laziness of the tideless Baltic. I'd forgotten that this sort of fun was supposed to involve sleep deprivation, discomfort and hypothermia. Happily I wasn't at the time aware that today was the planned start of the Fastnet race, which was postponed for a day for the first time in its history due to the forecast storms. I know that this corner of the German Bight is a long way from Southampton, but hundreds of boats retiring from the Fastnet is not what you want on your mind as you head out into a choppy North Sea.

After a splashy start motor sailing into a force 4 or 5 with wind over tide, as the sun came up the wind decreased, eventually down to nothing. The daylight meant I was better able to identify the owners of all the red, green and white lights that surrounded me – about 40 other yachts all heading west from Cuxhaven. I made 17 miles with the tide in the first two hours. In the event most of the 66 mile trip was spent in sunbathing mode, motoring over a flat sea.

An appealing bit of Teutonic eccentricity

Seaside towns like Teutonic Trumptons

I relied on my trusty PC and chartplotter as I approached the shifting sands of Norderney Island. I headed for where the main channel was and vaguely wondered where all the other boats were going and what those green and red buoys a mile or so off my course were. It was only when I'd made the entrance, on a falling half-tide at springs, that I realised that they were all heading for the same place as me. They had been following the buoys – which change position often as the channel shifts – as opposed to an old chart. I came out in a bit of a cold sweat at the realisation that I could easily have been 'neaped' and left on an exposed sandbank in the middle of the German Bight.

In the shallows behind Norderney was an entirely different set of craft to the seagoing yachts I'd been keeping company with. Wee shallow draft day boats and dinghies, catamarans and motor boats, sailing and anchored across the huge area of drying sands, waiting for the tide to go out to leave them on their little patch of temporary land for the evening.

Sunrise in the German Bight

Fishing off Norderney

I rafted up against a beautiful 45ft steel Dutch ketch and two other Dutch yachts rafted up outside me in the crowded harbour. Ashore I found this huge sand dune of an island to be an even more popular holiday spot than Cuxhaven. The beaches were thronged and the streets packed with bicycles, since the touros aren't allowed to bring their cars. With a fairly poor wee coastline 80 million or so Germen are determined to make the best use of it for sitting around on beaches.

The forecast for the following day suggested that the respite from strong westerlies had been brief. I decided to head into the Dutch canal system at the earliest opportunity and to head for Delfzijl. There are basically two ways of getting there: outside round Borkum Island, or the 'Riddle of the Sands' route across the massive drying area inside the islands. The latter option involved leaving at exactly eight a.m. and travelling at least 5.5 knots, without detour, so as to avoid being left high and dry by the retreating tide. Since the rest of the four boat raft was also doing this I decided on the inshore route.

The idea is that you head out early enough and follow the birch twigs stuck in the sand to mark the route. If you run aground on the way in that's OK, you just wait for more water then push on until you run aground again. I motored off into a grey and showery morning with 4 or 5 other boats. Though we were relatively early none of us ran aground and the depth never went below six foot as we followed the tortuous, winding course over the sands. After an hour or so I happened to look back and saw a quite surreal sight. Seemingly hundreds of boats of all types in a long snake winding its way along the twisting line of birch trees growing out of the sea. Most were yachts, but there were some of the shallow draft fishing boats with nets cantilevered out on long arms each side, which dipped into the shallow sea periodically to scrape the fish off the bottom. Most surreal in this area of drying sandbanks was the occasional quite large ship. Shallow draft ferries ply their trade to the islands across these drying puddles.

I was quite relieved eventually to get back into what passes for deep water in these parts; that is over about 1.5m at low tide. To celebrate I got the sails up

and reached into the estuary of the Ems. After a few torrential showers had passed over the sun came out, the wind died away and it turned into a sweltering day as we motored into Delfzijl harbour. After a five minute wait at the lock gate it opened and we locked once more into fresh water and the next major phase of the journey – the Dutch canal system.

Part 6 – Going Dutch

In Norderney I had laid my hands on what was to become my bible for the next wee while – the A4 book of charts for the Staande Masteroute all the way through the Netherlands. Of the thousands of potential routes through the Netherlands by canal this is the only route that doesn't involve sailing boats unstepping their masts. The term 'Staande Masteroute' hopefully needs no translation, but I could do with a linguist telling me why it's not called the 'Staandemaste Route'. My pilot book pronounced the first stage of this route – from Delfzijl to Groningen – as too dull, boring and time-consuming to be bothered with. It was however, with the exception of a half hour wait at a bridge on the outskirts of Groningen, fast, straight and easy, with relatively few bridges. With hindsight it was the easiest and quickest bit of my trip through the Dutch canals.

Arriving in Groningen I first rafted up on the only British yacht I'd seen since Rendsburg. I then noticed that the only reason to raft up was if you were large. Beside the rafts of big yachts was a half empty marina of narrow, piled, box moorings. There was, as usual, plenty of space for wee ones. I took a box mooring to complete a rather good 51 mile day.

The cruel and outlawed Dutch practice of 'Sprögdangling'

Pondering... I'd always thought that the multitude of urban canals were something special to Amsterdam which made it unique. I was now to find out that every town in the Netherlands, seemingly, is a maze of fantastically aesthetic little canals stuffed with boats of all descriptions, from old sailing barges to barely floating caravans. Groningen was very nice and twee, but by no means unique in this.

What did make Groningen unique was that its yoof festival was actually a success. I wandered the town later that night after it had been taken over by a huge stage pumping out dance music and a spectacular light show. This was evidently where all the yoof of northern Europe actually congregated. Thousands of student types thronged the streets. It was quite fun until I realised that I was the only person on the streets of Groningen over the age of 25.

I began to appreciate the speed with which we'd shot down the canal the previous day as I waited for over an hour for the first bridge to open on my way through Groningen. Once a small convoy of Belgian and French boats had built up we did get under way, but the 9 hour journey of 33 miles to Dokkum was slow going, with 26 bridges and a couple of locks to negotiate. The ideal way to approach the bridges is to be behind a larger, faster boat in a hurry. They zoom off ahead, alerting the bridge keeper to their approach and by the time you've arrived, at a more leisurely pace, the bridge is ready to open, minimising the hanging around and the trying to keep the boat stationary in a canal with a force six wind on the nose.

Groningen and your bog-standard Dutch canal scene

Traditional sailing barge

Pondering... Though we're used to calling The Netherlands 'Holland', the provinces of North and South Holland only make up a quarter of the country. Is Netherland/Holland the same as UK/England, or do the denizens of Groningen, Friesland and elsewhere not mind being told they are from Holland? I saw no evidence of seething resentment against Holland, though Friesland was filled with their odd flags adorned by a series of diagonal, upturned buttocks. During a long conversation with someone from Holland I was assured that really nobody at all in the Netherlands minds it being assumed they are from Holland. However, he ended with "there's a few Friesians who moan about it, but they are just radical loonies and we ignore them". Hmmm.

The journey through Groningen Province and Friesland is a picturesque and somewhat surreal one. If conditions are right you can sail, as opposed to motor, through the canals. A lot of quite large traditional Dutch sailing barges, as well as more conventional craft, choose to do so. Canals criss-cross the pancake flat landscape everywhere. As you sail past a herd of cows and a thatched rose-covered farmhouse, you'll see an eighty foot ship under full sail apparently sailing right across the field. The villages are all chocolate box images and twee to the point of obsession and were it not for the 25 knot cross winds and the completely crap autopilot, sailing through the canals would be a very relaxing experience.

Zoph sailed under jib where possible, with the engine on standby, but in these winding, tree lined canals I was constantly furling the jib to go to windward or applying a bit of throttle in the lulls through the trees. You're allowed to sail down all the canals, I think. The signs suggesting otherwise along some of them simply mean

that you have to have an engine running and ready to deploy. Having seen bugger all British boats through Scandinavia I spotted another two today – a sight that we were getting nearer to home waters, if you count the south of England as home waters.

> **Clogging...** *At a few points along the Staande Mastroute there are tolls to pay. Typically you'll pay between 2 and 6 Euros to go through the 5 or 6 bridges in a town. The system for collecting tolls is universal and surprising, demonstrating what I imagine to be Dutch humour and willingness to conform to their stereotype. As you pass through the first opening bridge in the town the bridge keeper hangs out of the control building above and dangles a sort of fishing rod down at you. Attached to a bit of string on the end of the rod is – you guessed it – a clog. An actual, miniaturised, traditional wooden Dutch clog. You bung your small change into the toe end and he whisks it away. If you don't spot the impending clogging soon enough it can be quite difficult steering the boat at 0.5 knots through a narrow bridge in a full gale on the beam, whilst at the same time trying to remove your wet weather gear to get at the change in your trouser pockets. This caught me out a couple of times, but happily without major mishap, unless you count people on other yachts taking the piss.*

Preparing for a clogging

Suburbs as twee as can be

Dokkum was another picture-postcard town criss-crossed by canals and again Zoph slotted nicely into one of the piled box moorings, while everyone else had to raft up. It's a problem faced by the Dutch that the piled mooring boxes are pretty permanent and fixed in size, whilst yachts have grown in length and particularly in beam. The 38ft Beneteau 'Mussolini', with its fourteen foot beam, just won't fit into any of the available spaces.

It was another 9 hour journey the next day to get the 37 miles from Dokkum to Sneek, possibly the best place name since Middlefart. Most of the way I was motoring in a full gale, though I did get in a bit of sailing under jib. The anemometer registered the highest wind speed of any passage so far, at 42 knots.

Sod's law dictated that when the engine overheating alarm started screeching I was in a bit of canal about 150 yards wide, with a full gale on the starboard beam and only reed beds and mud flats on either side. Of course I had ignored the change in engine note for the past half hour or so, putting it down to my usual paranoia.

What I should have done was motored to the weather shore and dropped the anchor or tried to throw it ashore before stopping the engine and clearing the water filter. What I actually did was stop the engine immediately and get fenders out on the port side, coming to rest against some rotting piling which was holding back the reed beds on the lee shore. Zoph scraped, bounced and dragged herself along the bits of rotting wood, since there was absolutely nothing to tie onto. I threw the kedge anchor into the reedbeds and that stopped her moving forward, but it was still uncomfortable and scratchy. I soon cleaned out the fishy smelling crap that gunged up the water filter, then addressed the problem of pushing off the lee shore. This I accomplished with some difficulty, further scratching and the loss of a fender, eventually being all-but left behind on the reedy swamp. I learnt that, as a general rule, it's a bad idea, whilst sailing single-handed, to open the throttle in forward gear then jump ashore. The damage done was only a few scratches, but the only hull damage of the trip and avoidable if I'd have had my wits about me and not been such a moron.

I managed a bit of a sail before arriving, as the wind abated a little. Sneek was billed in the pilot book as the world's single most gorgeous place. I couldn't see its attractions myself and had a less than perfect experience as I motored around the town's 3 large marinas looking for a berth. I finally found what was definitely the last available one of the thousand or so berths. To top a perfect day, the meal I ordered from the Dutch menu in the town turned out to be a huge pile of damp, stale nachos, clearly designed as a snack for an undiscerning rugby team on a piss up. Passers by pointed and stared as I struggled through the mountain of indigestible wet cardboard and reflected on what had been, all in all, a relatively poor sort of day.

Pondering... *One of the positive things about the Dutch waterways is the behaviour of the motor boats. I started out in Norway, where I was constantly having to battle through the breaking wakes of innumerable ruddy great motorboats*

struggling to get their enormous bulks up to planing speed. In Dutch waters I hardly had a wake to contend with as, with a very few exceptions, gin palaces, speedboats, barges and sailing boats alike stuck obligingly to the speed limit. I'm told a recent crack-down on speedsters has helped.

I hoped for a better day as I headed for Lemmer the following morning in a gusty south-westerly force 5 to 6. As the canal system opened out into a series of shallow lakes I unfurled the jib and we had a cracking sail at up to 6.5 knots on a fine reach. This included one of those races you have where the opposition don't necessarily know they are in a race and if you lose you weren't really racing. Suffice to say I beat the wee Beneteau, so we were racing.

Though I kept to the middle of the channel, shallower draft local boats, with better local knowledge, used the full width of the lakes for sailing and mooring.

Pondering... Like in Norway everywhere was well equipped with places to moor, with little signs saying mooring was free for up to 72 hours, in places providing toilets and waste disposal. All very civilised and I slightly regretted the fact that I really had to press on and didn't have time to loiter at all the nicest pastoral spots.

After only 14 miles I arrived in the attractive old main street of Lemmer, where I rafted up against a charter yacht in what at first looked like a good spot. There's usually a good reason why places are available however and I soon realised we were on a blind corner just next to a lifting bridge, where boats had to do complex manoeuvres to avoid being blown to the side of the canal whilst they waited. Still, I decided to stay, since the middle of town was pleasant and the various marinas, with berths for thousands of boats, were a bit windswept and out in the suburbs.

Your typical Dutch bird. Very tall you'll notice

Pondering... Lemmer had some a good examples of a Dutch irony – the suburban canal estate. For hundreds of years – famously – the Dutch have painstakingly reclaimed much of their country from the sea and marsh. Over the centuries, largely with back-breaking human effort, they have built dykes and polders and created fertile farmland out of sea and tidal swamp. Generation upon generation of farmers have dedicated their lives to creating this land.

Then, about a week last Tuesday, most Dutch people stopped being farmers and got 40ft yachts. Obviously they would like their yachts to be parked just outside their houses or, if at all possible, inside their houses. So if you are a suburban housing developer the first thing you need to do to make a new suburb saleable is send in the JCBs and dig half the land up, flooding it in a series of canals designed only to park yachts outside houses. Since a lot of Dutch yachts are – surprisingly given the sheltered waters in which they sail – pretty serious ocean going steel affairs, this creates a rather surreal sight. Rows of Barratt houses next to each of which is parked, alongside the family Ford Focus, a world-girdling Cape Horn yacht. Meanwhile the ghosts of all the old farmers wonder why they bothered filling in all the wet bits.

In Lemmer I was invited aboard a small traditional old Dutch sailing barge for a drink. Squatting down below in the dark wooden interior with about 3 ft of headroom they told me about their boat. Built 100 years ago she was only about 30ft, with a draft of 18 inches and no ballast, yet according to her skipper she weighed 10 tonnes. With their square shape, bluff bows and characteristic curved gaffs they don't look fantastically sleek or fast, but there is a charm and workmanlike aesthetic to these old barges.

Rain heavy enough to flatten 6ft waves

Rafted up in Lemmer

Pondering... Whilst most Scandinavians are content to zap about in the fastest new boat they can afford, a lot of Dutch people seem to take the boat owning hobby pretty seriously. You'd have to if you took on the maintenance involved in owning a hundred year old wooden ship. As I travelled further south there were more and more of these boats. Nearly all in immaculately varnished and polished condition and ranging from about 30ft to huge creaky two mast-ers of eighty or ninety foot. Many of them seem to be owned by trusts and charities and are probably, like my chum in Lemmer's boat, listed ancient monuments. Honestly. Their thirty foot yacht *was a listed historical monument, which meant that they got even cheaper berthing than anyone else, amongst other things. You wouldn't know we were supposed to be a nation of seafarers when you see how much more seriously the rest of Europe takes its maritime traditions.*

The next morning I locked out of Lemmer and into the Ijsselmeer, the Zijder Zee as was. I started out beating under full sail, then I put in two reefs in the main as the wind increased, then I motored under reefed main only into the teeth of a force 6 and quite possibly the most torrential rain I had ever seen. It rained hard enough to flatten the sea, even with a 15 mile fetch and a force 6. Happily, being out in the open water meant I could leave the wind vane steering (Leo) to its own devices and avoid getting soaked for periods.

Pondering... There seems to be some controversy about why the Zijder Zee was turned into a freshwater lake. Was it to control flooding by the sea, or allow navigation for ships, or help the fishing, or begin to drain it and turn it into farmland, or just to make a nice big lake? It seems to depend on who is telling the story.

There were few other yachts about, but plenty of commercial barges, until I approached the lock into the Markermeer at Enkhuizen. As we entered the lock the rain had stopped and things were brightening up, but it was still blowing hard and difficult to get a line ashore. In the waiting area for the lock was the third Vancouver enthusiast I had encountered abroad. A guy sailing a wooden folkboat with his wife who recognised Zoph as a Vancouver, kindly helped with the lines and waxed gratifyingly lyrical.

The huge, new concrete lock had just been built for the use of leisure craft. Though a fraction of the size of the parallel commercial locks, it was large enough for about a hundred yachts and as big as all the canal locks in Scotland put together. It is certainly as big a structure as anything built in Scotland in the past fifty years or so. Unusually, there were actual people operating the lock and, to make sure I had enough line out I asked one of them whether we were locking up or down. She said she wasn't sure if we would go up or down, but thought it was about 3 centimetres. I repeat: the person employed to operate the lock didn't know if it would go up or down. Millions of euros of new civil engineering to go up or down an inch.

Pondering... Dutch Locks aren't, of course, like ours. They don't aim to lift boats up hills but are there for flood control, so the direction of locking may change. It is often the case in Holland, as in the Kiel canal, that you are surprised to find yourself locking up into the sea, instead of down.

After Enkhuizen the wind moderated to eighteen to twenty four knots apparent so I got up full sail and had a very pleasant sail close hauled in hot sunshine towards Edam, with only the need for a couple of short tacks at the end. With the sun out came hundreds of boats of all descriptions, including lots of traditional sailing barges. Since this is a large chunk of water practically all the boats were sailing boats, which made a nice change after days in the company of a mixed bag of motorboats.

Entering the canal at Edam I passed a couple of small British trailer-sailers which had come over on the ferry from Hull. What an excellent way of seeing Holland that would be, avoiding the stress of waiting about for a weather window to cross the North Sea twice. Few Brits seem to have thought of this excellent way of cruising in either the Netherlands or Norway. I locked into Edam and was told that there was one more lock before the town. However, though I waited at it for an hour or so, the lock keeper never arrived to open it. According to some very pissed people on a barge, he was most likely pissed himself at the start of some sort of massive cheese- and-booze-related Edam shin-dig.

So I moored outside the lock, but pretty near the middle of town, in a tiny space between two huge two masted hundred foot sailing ships, their bowsprits practically passing through Zoph's rigging. It was so calm in amongst the trees here that she might as well have been set in concrete. Later on a wizened old Harbour Master turned up and asked for harbour dues. A bit rich I thought since I wasn't really in a harbour. He pointed out that the bogs and showers were 2 miles away down the canal, but said that when it comes to pooing I might as well just use the canal since the fish need something to eat.

Pooing... This attitude to pooing, in an enclosed stretch of narrow canal about a mile long, surprised me a little, but the Dutch do seem rather casual about such things. I expected a heavily populated country in which everyone's got a boat and all are sailing in shallow, narrow, tideless inland waters, to be sticklers for holding tanks and pumping out. My lack of a holding tank was one of the reasons why I'd not moored for the night in any wild places, away from the villages. From conversations with a number of people it became apparent that, if there's a bog ashore they'll use it, if not, a few million poos never did anyone any harm. They are also quite keen, oddly, on swimming.

As luck would have it I was moored in Edam right next to the stop for buses from Amsterdam, an important consideration as the Shoreside Logistics Team was due to join me for a long weekend. The vague plan that had emerged was to do a weekend's cheese tour, through the canals from Edam to Gouda. I wandered round the almost painfully pictureskew old town looking at the tweenery while I waited.

A cheesy scene in Edam

Bring and buy Edam style

Of course the Shoreside Logistics Team got on the wrong bus and I had to fetch Anna from miles away, but she was nevertheless impressed by the old houses and shops crowded round the maze of tiny canals. The morning revealed the world's largest and most futile bring and buy sale. Every inch of every street in Edam was covered in tables and sheets on the ground, in turn overflowing with an assortment of old and broken tat. Everyone in Edam had a stall and were all trying to sell their broken skateboards, jigsaw puzzles with bits missing and early '80s clothes to each other. It was virtually impossible to get from one end of the street to the other, such was people's enthusiasm to squint at other people's discarded rubbish. In common with other 'festivals' this summer, the main point seemed to be to wander aimlessly in long crocodiles looking at stuff, then go home. Still, it was all a bit of local colour.

Pondering... We visited the town museum, sited in a 15th century merchant's house which had solved the problem of flooding and changing water levels by having a basement which was actually floating on the groundwater. The angles at which the walls on these old houses lean seem to defy gravity and are a reminder that you are in the precarious environment of a boggy swamp below sea level. Having a basement that is actually floating serves to reinforce the precariousness of living, like those creatures on Stingray, below sea level. As far as I could tell however, the Dutch do not have gills.

After a leisurely morning and lunch we set out in the afternoon for a very pleasant beat in a force 3 the short distance to Marken. On the way we passed hundreds of yachts, including many more traditional barges with tan sails. We were hailed by a bloke on one of them, who wanted to know where we were from. He was impressed that we'd come from Scotland, where he used to live. It was all very pleasant and friendly in the sunshine.

Sailing in the
Markermeer

We took a box mooring in Marken harbour and went for a wander in the sun. Marken is an ex-island, now joined to the mainland by a causeway. We had a nice meal and a few beers by the harbour watching the sun go down and, unfortunately, listening to shouting pissed tourists and loud crap MOR American music.

> *Pondering… The pilot book had the locals down as right inbred yokels and we were half expecting duelling banjos, but in the event I think it's more-or-less a commuter suburb of Amsterdam now. The older house are all built in tight clusters on man made hills around the island. A legacy of the days when it used to flood regularly. Everywhere is looking quite yuppified now, but very pleasant.*

Surprisingly, the next day also dawned sunny. Surely we couldn't be getting two and a half days of summer all in a row! Destination Hamsterjam and again a slightly surreal experience to sail through farmland and suburbs into the middle of a big city. We ran down the side of Marken then beat round it into a force 2 to 3, easing off to a fine reach to sail in a lot of company down to Amsterdam. We didn't sail right into the city like some local folk, but got the sails down early and motored through the bridges and on to the large locks that protect the city. We motored on to the Sixhaven marina, which we had been warned could be packed to the gunwales, as the nearest berthing to the city centre, but in the event was only three quarters full. Apparently the School hols had finished. Sixhaven is right opposite the central railway station and though the wrong side of the river from the centre, has a free 24 hour ferry service running from quite close by.

In the evening we did a whistle-stop tour of the main sights of Amsterdam on foot and had quite a posh meal. Nice though Hamsterjam is, we were getting a bit blasé about twee towns with intricate networks of aesthetic canals and decided to leave any detailed sightseeing to a future trip by Easyjet from Edinburgh. We went back on board Zoph disgracefully early, leaving other more metropolitan types to the nightlife and debauchery.

Another sunny day dawned, this time with no wind. We headed west through the main shipping channel and the Nordzeekanaal towards Ijmuiden, aiming to turn left after six or seven miles, first stop Haarlem. In the event the 13

miles to Haarlem took all of 12
hours. The second bridge on the
Zykanaal has restricted opening
hours and we'd left in plenty of
time to catch the mid day opening.
Unfortunately - we were informed
by people on a couple of Dutch
yachts waiting at the pontoon - the
first bridge was broken and wasn't
going to open. We tied up on the
stagings provided - which were fine

A Dutch suburb

for mooring but didn't provide any route ashore - and waited. And waited. And
waited. After about 3 hours an engineer appeared. After about half an hour he
went away again, having brought the wrong key to get into the workings of the
bridge. An hour later he reappeared and diagnosed a problem with the
hydraulics, disappearing again to go and get a part.

Altogether we waited for 7 hours, from 10.30 am to 5.30 pm, for the bridge to
open. Then we waited for 2 hours, until 7.30, for the second, motorway bridge to
open. Eventually we all passed into Haarlem in convoy. Someone had told us
that the best place to stop was after the third bridge in the middle of Haarlem.
We duly did this, while the rest of the convoy carried on and stopped after the
4th bridge in the proper place to moor. A curse on innumerate Dutch people.

Haarlem was pleasant enough however and we were able to do a small pub
crawl through the town and get slightly pissed before bed time, which can't be
bad.

> **Pondering...** *Along with clogs and windmills, you'd expect Holland to be thick
> with bicycles. It is and Haarlem was no exception. Denmark and Germany are also
> pretty biked up, but there was something quintessentially different and Dutch about
> the bikes in Holland which at first I couldn't put my finger on. Then I realised that
> your Dutch cyclist is just more laid back, literally. The bikes look strangely alien
> somehow. They manufacture them with just a bit higher handlebars and longer,
> more rakish front forks. It gives the bikes a slightly haughty, superior expression and
> makes the cyclists sit up straight, head in the air, even leaning backwards slightly.
> Since there's no hills of course, they can afford this posture, which gives the
> impression of never having to put any effort in. It is a stark contract to the
> demeanour of your Scottish cyclist, bent double over the handlebars and struggling
> up a hill against a headwind.*

They are both literally and figuratively more laid back. In Germany
everyone seems obsessively to follow the rules of the road – waiting for the little
green man to start beeping and so on. Holland is more refreshingly anarchic,
with hordes of laid back cyclists criss-crossing one another seamlessly at all sorts

of angles. In Haarlem, for example, we saw a young couple cycling through the town at 11 in the evening, him making a phone call whilst holding a glass of wine and her drinking a cup of coffee.

Given the slow progress the previous day it became obvious that we weren't going to make Gouda in time for Anna to get back to Schiphol for her flight. We were going to have to curtail our cheese tour. We decided to head for Alphen ad Rijn, which was on the route and had a mainline train station. On the way we passed a series of calm, shallow lakes on which dinghies and shoal draft cruisers drifted in the sun. All very pleasant, but as usual we had to press on – no time for drifting – and didn't really have enough local information to risk a short-cut through the shallow lakes.

We did manage a bit of gentle sailing across the Braassemermeer before arriving in the town centre of Alphen ad Rijn. The wind had got up a bit and made the canal a tad choppy. This, coupled to the local neds whizzing round and round in circles in open boats with noisy outboards, actually made tying up on the canal rather uncomfortable for Zoph.

A Dutch mast-trimmer

Cliche or what?

Anna left by train for Schiphol and I headed off again with Zoph, aiming for Gouda. I passed through a series of bridges of different design to the ones we'd thus far come across. Huge tall steel lattice towers either side of the canal with a road in a lattice girder between them. The whole road winches up the towers and you pass beneath it. Unlike the other bridge designs, this is slightly fraught as you try to judge whether the bridge has risen high enough to whiz through yet. To someone on the bank it was probably obvious that there was loads of clearance, but from the deck the masthead appears to be scraping the bottom of the bridge.

The last bridge into Gouda was a bit of a bugger. It is a rail bridge with limited opening times and, with half a mile to go, I had to wait until 9 pm for it to open. While waiting and in the gathering gloom I decided to check the fuel, using Zoph's sophisticated fuel gauge – a bit of clear plastic pipe stuck in the bottom of the tank and tied up its side. I was distressed to find that we only had 2 gallons left in the 30 gallon tank. How could I have used so much since the last fill in Dokkum? Anyway I clearly needed more. I emptied the 25 litre spare can into the tank to be going on with.

I arrived at the rather low-key Gouda marina in pitch dark and pissing down rain. Under the direction of the harbour master I rafted up against a big motor cruiser. I asked if I could get fuel in the morning and received a series of tut-tuts, shakings of the head and looks of disbelief. He explained that, because of European legislation it was virtually impossible to buy diesel anywhere in Holland and he certainly had no idea where it was available within a hundred miles or so. I pointed out that there were several million boats all powered by diesel engines and that they must get fuel somewhere. He agreed that this did seem odd but reiterated that it was impossible to buy fuel in the Netherlands. I took a wander towards the town centre, but it turned out to be miles away and pissing down, so I gave up and retired.

Dortrecht

Willemstad

The next morning I thought I'd just check the fuel again, for some reason. I found that there was about 20 gallons, with about 7 gallons of red diesel at the bottom and 13 gallons of clear stuff, which is what you buy in Denmark and Holland, floating on top of it. In the gloom the previous evening I'd been looking at the line of red diesel and not been able to see the clear stuff. I don't know if the red diesel is heavier, or if it's actually the dye that concentrates at the bottom when it's sufficiently diluted.

Beyond Gouda I was in a river system. This was broader and rougher than the canals and increasingly more industrial the further south we went. I motored then motorsailed in company of a Dutch Trintella 29 which I'd seen a few times in the last couple of days. We went down the Ijssel in a force five from the North East. We had to hang about for a good while in breezy, choppy conditions before locking through into the wider, breezier and much busier Noord. There were few yachts, but a constant procession of ships and commercial barges.

After being useless for as long as I could remember, then playing up and being worse than useless, the electronic tillerpilot finally packed up altogether. This was a relief in a way, since I'd been looking for an excuse to buy one that actually worked. On the other hand it made steering down the rest of the Dutch canal system a little tedious. The wind vane self steering (called Leo as that's what you shout when it's steering you to come about) helped a lot but was not ideal for narrow canals under motor.

Since we were just in a canal I'd left a couple of fenders hanging over the side, but since we were sailing with some heel and I'm an idiot and hadn't attached the fenders properly, I looked behind to see one floating off in the distance. I furled the jib, did a quick spin and went back to fetch it. Unfortunately there was a strong crosswind and it very quickly blew up against the bank, lined with rusty steel piles 15 feet high. After a couple of goes at retrieving it in quite choppy, windy conditions, I decided that the loss of a small and anyway rather crappy wee fender was less of a blow than would have been major damage to the hull so, feeling rather foolish, I left it behind.

Crane, bridge and cathedral at Dortrecht

Mooring on Lake Veere

As chance would have it a large seagoing tug, of the kind that shunts oil tankers about, was passing and they obviously noticed my sad loss. The tug turned round, motored back down the river, went alongside the piles and, with some difficulty, retrieved my fender. They motored over to Zoph and flung the fender over to me, receiving my craven and embarrassed gratitude. Heartwarming human story or what?

Due to the rather confusing fact that the current flows eastwards, away from the sea, all the time here, we soon arrived in Dortrecht. Here there is another bridge with restricted opening times, so I tied up on a rather exposed and choppy visitors' pontoon and had a quick look at the town, with it's startlingly Pisaesque leaning cathedral. Presumably it's slowly sinking into the mire. All my attempts to photograph it with its list were in vain since it always just looked like I was slightly pissed and couldn't hold the camera straight. We went through this huge lifting bridge in the company of the Trintella, a larger yacht and a huge crane barge, its lattice structure rivalling the massive towers of the bridge. There's a lot of big civil engineering in Holland.

Soon after we were spat out into the wide and windy open space of Noord Hollandsch Deep, formerly a large estuary and now an inland lake and a major shipping lane. In the open waters I got full sail up and we ran down the remaining 8 miles to Willemstad at 6 knots, beating the Trintella easily, which was nice, if unexpected.

The marina at Willemstad was nearly full but I managed to get a tight box mooring then walked over the ramparts to the old town. The marina is in a sort of moat which formed part of the star shaped fortifications of yet another extraordinarily twee little town, once again a popular holiday spot.

> **Pondering...** *Like most wee Dutch towns Willemstad seems to benefit, in a way, from the fact that it's had absolutely nothing going for it since about the 16th century. These towns were built on trade when they were viable coastal ports with relatively tiny ships plying the wool trade and so forth. Having been rendered pretty well useless for hundreds of years by reclamation and changes in the coast, their industrial landscape is that of twee canals and posh merchants' houses hundreds of years old. Ideal material for aesthetic little pretend market towns which are actually posh suburbs.*

Most Scottish towns have a similarly salubrious past, with fine old buildings and an infrastructure built for trade. Unfortunately, most of them had their heyday in Victorian times and the early part of the twentieth century. There is rather less call, as yet, to make salubrious suburbs out of the dockland environment of Greenock or Kirkcaldy, despite their fine Victorian buildings. So if you are going to fail economically, make sure you do it a very long time ago.

Willemstad fitted this model particularly well and is an absurdly twee little fortified town. Doubtless very annoying to live in, since there's about 12 restaurants and a large chandler but not, as far as I could tell, anywhere to buy a pint of milk.

Outside Willemstad the next morning I locked into the Noord Volkerak, another bit of ex-estuary that's now separated from the sea by a dam, through another massive lock with room for about 100 yachts. This was of course just the wee yacht lock, not one of the three proper ship locks. I tried sailing under full sail for an hour or so, but on a dead run in a force 1 it was a bit fruitless so I joined loads of other boats motorsailing in the sun across the flat calm water. We all accelerated to try and jump the queue into the next, equally big lock. Zoph's mainsail being incredibly hard to raise and lower, I had to turn to windward to lower it while everyone else motored straight in to the lock. I had to wait half an hour for the next locking into the tidal Oosterschelde, the first bit of salt water for ten days

After motoring west I turned south onto a reach so managed full sail up to the next lock and the entrance to Veere lake. Veere is about as long as the Forth west of the bridges and about half as wide, with bugger all local population. It has about 20 marinas, each with around 500 boats and I stopped for the night at one of the first, a rather posh big affair filled with gin palaces near the village of Kortgene. A cycle to the village and a meal rounded off a good sort of day.

Summer had really arrived - on August 24th – and as I motored down the beautiful pastoral lake the next morning, past pontoons on tiny wee reed covered islands, I rather regretted having stopped in a very commercial marina the previous night. I stopped for late breakfast at a pontoon on the tiny island of Zandkreekplaat, mooring in a tight space between two small Belgian yachts. I dived in for what I realised was my first (and last) swim of the summer, then walked all the way round the island in about a minute and a half. Hot sun, not a breath of wind and a more or less deserted island, except for a crowd of very friendly Belgians whose boats I had moored between. We had a long chat about just how bizarre they thought it was that I'd come there from Scotland.

> **Pondering...** *On diving in to lake Veere I was surprised to find that the water was salty, given that it's above sea level and surrounded by reclaimed farm land. My Belgian chums explained that it used to be fresh water but there wasn't enough of it so the Dutch had to pump salt water up into it to keep it a viable lake. I still don't quite get what the agenda is for land reclamation in Holland. They do seem to make life extraordinarily difficult for themselves.*

Not having far to go and not being in a hurry for once I stopped in the town of Veere as well. Apparently built on the wool trade with Scotland, this was yet another picture-perfect medieval theme town and, of course, a popular holiday spot. An ice cream later I headed south east in the baking sun, locking through into a small and less busy canal that led to Middelburg. Reputed to be worth a visit, I pulled into the first empty box mooring in the town, intending to check out with the harbour master if it was OK.

Veere

Whilst I was tying up, a fat and pompous man drew up sweating on a bicycle and asked 'are you Mr Brown?'. I answered that I wasn't and that he must be looking for someone else. He replied with something like 'what makes you think you can just tie up there, who do you think you are, Mr Brown?' The penny dropped in my slow brain and I realised that this was humour and he was being a sarcastic bastard. For some reason Gordon Brown would be allowed to moor here, because he is important, but I was not. I realised I was talking to the harbour master, who directed me impatiently to another part of town to berth. Though in some ways being treated like shit did make me think of home waters, I'd not had this sort of welcome anywhere else and was a little dumbfounded. After brief reflection I cast off, reversed out of the berth and told him he could stick Middelburg up his arse as I motored off towards Vlissingen. This was the first instance of any sort of unfriendliness in a harbour in 5 countries.

Pondering... The fact that Vlissingen is called by the British 'Flushing' sounds like it might be a vague insult. Perhaps generations of Brits have been abused by harbour masters in Middelburg, which does sort of flush out into the sea at Flushing. However most Dutch people don't seem to mind it being called Flushing.

When I was flushed through Flushing there was a massive festival of the sea going on and the harbour was packed to the gunwales with tall ships of every description. I tried to photograph them – with little success - as I dodged through the middle on the way to the sea lock and they manoeuvred around the harbour. There were seemingly hundreds of tall ships in the dock, thousands of onlookers thronging the sides and millions of flags and bits of bunting flying in the hot afternoon sun.

I just squeezed into the last space in the lock and the crew of a chunky, beamy sixty foot fishing boat took my lines as we rafted up. For once this lock actually took us downwards to sea level and about half way down the fishing boat got her starboard side caught on an underwater cill and leaned alarmingly over towards Zoph. Then she slipped off the cill and had us both careering across the lock. A near disaster but no harm done.

Outside Flushing harbour it was definitely real sea again, with a distinct chop from the north west. It was only a couple of miles across the estuary to the large and organised marina at Breskens, where I had a little difficulty rafting up on a big Beneteau in the increasing wind. The marina was completely stuffed with boats, since every racer and cruiser-racer for a hundred miles round had turned up for the event of the year, Breskens regatta weekend. There were a lot of big posh racing yachts with rather snooty crews, with their wrap around shades and Kevlar and carbon fibre this, that and the other.

> **Pondering**... *Zoph was moored next to a 45ft Trintella called Antares. I saw they had a 'Rolex Fastnet' sticker and asked if they'd been in the Fastnet race and if it had been a rough sort of experience. Not only had they been in it but they'd won their class. They also must have been shifting some to get all the way here afterwards. It was only 10 days since the start of the 600 mile race. I later discovered that another of the 60 or so boats to finish the race, from which about three quarters retired, was my cousin Stan in a Sigma 38 crewed by his daughters.*

Zoph's route through the Dutch canals and past Belgium

Part 7 – Beautiful Belgium (probably)

With a north westerly force 5 forecast for the next major sojourn into the wild North Sea I was again lucky to get increasingly cloudless skies, a hot summer day and nothing more than a force 2 or 3 on the nose for the 55 mile motorsail west south west to Dunkirque. It was a Sunday and the racing boats were out in force from all the ports on the route, Zeebrugge, Oostende and Niewpoort. There were large fleets of them everywhere, mostly drifting slowly in the gentle breeze.

It was, as you know if you sail on the Forth, one of Sod's laws that the Rosyth to Zeebrugge ferry was always heading down the main channel just as you want to cross it, and Sod made no exception as I crossed the channel into Zeebrugge just before midday, narrowly avoiding the ferry. I wondered how many return trips they would make to the Forth before Zoph encountered them again.

As I crossed the border into Belgian waters I assiduously lowered the Dutch flag and raised the Belgian one with due fanfare. About seven hours later I lowered it again and raised the French flag.

Vlissingen/Flushing

Pondering... What a waste of money that was. I should have used the German flag on its side. They ought to price flags according to the length of coastline of the country they belong to. The flag was the most expensive thing about my brief sojourn in Belgium.

Sunday sailing off Oostende

Part 8 – Vive La France

Dunkirque has a few serviceable but unlovely marinas and I got a pontoon in one of them and explored the town which looks, in common with most British commercial ports, like it's seen better days. The other thing it has in common with British ports is the marina fees. Well, not quite. Nowhere is as expensive as Britain, but Breskens and Dunkirque were doing me a favour by gently working up towards the astronomical berthing fees I was soon going to have to pay. At 10 in the evening the sky erupted with a major firework display which went on for about an hour. Very impressive and I had a front row seat in Zoph's cockpit.

My cunning plan of sidling round the coast of mainland Europe in order to head north west to the UK and take advantage of the prevailing south westerlies was foiled again by the forecast northerly breezes. However it was only blowing a force 3 and not quite on the nose as I motorsailed with the tide towards Ramsgate. Where there was a cross-tide it was a little choppy and splashy, but perfectly pleasant.

I negotiated three traffic separation zones with the help of the AIS and the chartplotter, which at times showed Zoph as a dot in the middle of hundreds of ships. The only thing that came relatively close however was a Russian shooty-ship which didn't, as one might have expected, appear on the AIS. Presumably the military have special dispensation not to let people know where they are.

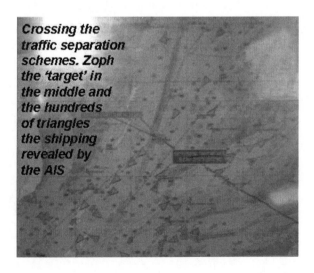

Crossing the traffic separation schemes. Zoph the 'target' in the middle and the hundreds of triangles the shipping revealed by the AIS

Part 9 – Drear Old Blighted

Though not exactly a homecoming, it was a bit of a milestone seeing the grey-green cliffs of Dover and Ramsgate and getting rid of all the National flags as we entered home waters. I used the VHF for the first time in months, as the port of Ramsgate apparently insists on all vessels calling up to leave or enter the harbour. They believe themselves to be a busy port, with their two ships a day, both of which are timetabled. It was faintly ridiculous listening to the posh voice giving permission for hundreds of yachts, creelboats, speedboats, dinghies, canoes and surfboards to leave the harbour for 5 minutes.

It was a hot summer afternoon in Ramsgate and all the fun of the fair was on the water, as the local lifeboat playfully showered everyone with its fire hoses. After finding a pontoon I went ashore and cycled round the town.

> *Pondering... After travelling round northern Europe it comes as no surprise that Britain heads the prestigious obesity league table. Nearly everyone in Ramsgate was pretty much the shape of a barrel. It was fairly difficult to tell where the head, neck and shoulders began and ended. You could tell where their arms started, because these were invariably tattooed and hanging onto a Rottweiler or other breed of attack dog. They waddled the streets in their thousands with their dogs, queuing round the block for fish and chips, ice cream and pints. I don't know if these people were actually the indigenous inhabitants of Ramsgate (who are presumably called Ramsgits). I suspect they might have been chirpy east end Cock-er-neys, replete with jellied eels and down for the holiday weekend. A couple of streets back from the seafront the town was run down, with buildings boarded up and the aspiring restaurants more or less empty. This suggested a very seasonal popularity for the seaside town.*

The greyish cliffs of Ramsgate

Security guards patrolled the harbour wall as a group of pyrotechnic hippies set up another firework display. Back on board I watched as the fireworks went off again at 9 o'clock in another hour long display to rival Dunkirque's. The rival displays were doubtless some sort of English v French thing going back to the Napoleonic Wars.

The following day culminated in a dramatic offer of rescue by the Coastguard, which I bravely refused. But more of that later.

After refuelling with red diesel the posh voice gave me permission to leave the wide open, deserted outer harbour. I had a really good beat for the first 4

hours across the Thames estuary
into a force 4 north westerly with
the tide. After a while however
the wind died, then came back
more   due   northerly,
necessitating a motorsail for
most of the rest of the way to
Harwich. The pilot book refers to
this bit of water as the second
most popular sailing area in
Britain. Aside from the fact that
it's near a major centre of

Lightships moored in Harwich harbour

population it's difficult to see why. It's also hard to appreciate the magical
quality of the scenery claimed by a lot of the sailing press for this pancake flat
set of drying mud banks, with nuclear power stations and cooling towers for
landmarks. There's nothing terribly unpleasant about it, just that a southern-
centred media has talked the area up way more than it deserves. It makes you
appreciate the Forth more for the good cruising ground it is.

> ***Pondering...*** *Much of the hyperbole came from the pilot book, astonishingly
> misnamed "East Coast Pilot". This "East Coast Pilot" covers the area from
> Ramsgate to Lowestoft, or two of my short day sails - 88 miles in all. It covers about
> 12% of the east coast yet is not called "The Far Southern 12% of the East Coast of
> Britain Pilot", which would be more accurate. This reflects the astonishing
> parochiality of your southern English yachtsman and long may it continue, leaving
> the decent cruising grounds relatively empty for the rest of us.*

I motorsailed up the Orwell, past Harwich and Felixstowe, past the four
bright red old light ships moored there, to the Suffolk Yacht harbour at
Levington, a rambling, scruffy and rather pleasant marina dug out of the drying
mud flats on the north bank. I walked the couple of miles to the local pub,
apparently famous for its meals, and indeed got quite decent scran at an outside
table.

On my return I stopped for a pint at the clubhouse of the local yacht club, in
an old converted red lightship. Though a scruffy sort of place this is yachting for
Londoners and there's plenty of money about. I listened for a while to a
depressing conversation between two well heeled but sad old business men,
each bemoaning the fact that their wives were being very unfair to their new
'girlfriends'.

I then asked for another pint.

> ***Pondering...*** *At this point I would urge anyone reading this to boycott this
> yacht club if in the area and preferably campaign to get them drummed out of the
> RYA. I produced a Bank of Scotland tenner to pay for my pint and was told by the*

barmaid, incredibly, that the Yacht Club Committee had convened a meeting at which it had been resolved that no one at the club was allowed to take any Scottish money. In 30 years of living in Scotland and occasionally spending money in England, this has only happened to me once before, at the hands of an overtly racist Brummie taxi driver. But this was the decision of a committee after sober reflection and taking a vote. I was outraged and incensed with fury at two things. Firstly, at this abomination of a club and its bigoted committee and secondly at me, for instead of sticking two fingers up and telling them to stick their light ship where the sun doesn't shine, I guddled about in my pocket for English money and paid for the pint. I still cringe with shame.

A good day and a pleasant evening was turned to shit by these stupid people.

Oh yes – the dramatic Coastguard rescue. While I was walking to the pub a Coastguard Landrover stopped and they asked if I wanted a lift anywhere, which was very nice of them. However they were going the wrong way and I declined the lift and therefore declined the dramatic Coastguard rescue.

The next day I headed out of the river against the tide and turned north along the coast of East Anglia. Again we had gentle northerlies, this time with a bit of east in it, so more motorsailing I'm afraid. As the tide turned in my favour I made very good progress, with 2.5 knots of favourable tide for long periods as I passed the featureless coast, punctuated by a couple of Suffolk villages looking quite pleasant in the sun.

Arriving in Lowestoft harbour I rafted up in the Royal Norfolk and Suffolk Yacht Club against an old wooden sloop populated by 4 Geordie blokes and went to speak to the marina staff about the possibility of leaving Zoph for a week or two. The yacht club had pretensions to gentility and there was obviously plenty of money about on the pontoons. It also had high security gates to keep the poor people out, something I was having to get used to again in Britain, having seen very little security elsewhere.

The marina staff were friendly but extraordinarily casual and just said I should leave her rafted up. The rafts of boats on the visitors pontoons moved on pretty much every day and apparently someone would shift Zoph and probably tie her up OK. This I didn't like the sound of, so Brompted the couple of miles inland to Lowestoft Haven Marina, a new facility with good substantial pontoons, but half empty in the run down stretch of river running inland towards the broads and filled with the rotting hulks of old ships.

A landmark. Rare in East Anglia

Pondering... *A cycle round Lowestoft revealed a deeply depressed town which didn't seem to manage to retain the seaside* *prosperity of its continental counterparts. Even the pound shops were closing down due to lack of business. Scenes like the three generations of women sitting outside on a dirt road to catch the sun, the door of their windowless backstreet hovel open to let in a bit of air as they choked on the dust thrown up by passing trucks, left a strong impression. The impression is of somewhere like Somalia, as opposed to the theoretically prosperous south of England. I do believe that a Dutch yachtsman, for instance, making landfall here and used, obviously, to small Dutch towns, would be genuinely shocked by the level of apparent deprivation in the world's 5th richest economy.*

After joining the Geordie blokes for a pint I went to bed and rose at nine the next morning to take Zoph through the lifting bridge to the other marina. This bridge only opens at prearranged times and not at rush hour, so I had opted for the 9.45 opening. This stretch of water connects a well travelled coast with the famous Norfolk Broads and as such you might think it would be quite a swish and well used waterway. I'm sure the Broads are very pleasant, but this route into them has the feel of a nautical graveyard. Atmospheric but sad..

I left Zoph on one of the many huge, brand new pontoons available, next to a Moody 54 from Guernsey and cycled to the station, where I took out a second mortgage to buy a ticket home. Work, I'm afraid, intruded for a couple of weeks.

Pondering... Most of the east coast of England is a surprisingly rubbish cruising ground. From Lowestoft (or at least Great Yarmouth) northwards there's bugger all places to go that aren't shallow drying creeks. The Humber is an option, but to get anywhere you have to go about 20 miles up the estuary, then of course 20 miles out again. The first place with more or less all tides access, where you don't dry out, is Whitby, some 150 miles from Lowestoft.

150 miles is way beyond my single handed day-sailing range, so I needed crew. A plea through the Port Edgar email group brought a couple of volunteers (thanks Fiona and Andy), but coordinating availability with weather proved difficult. So it was that I drew on the shoreside logistics team for support and Anna joined me on the train down to Lowestoft to undertake her first night

Sunset looking towards the Humber

watches. The considerable downside of this was that I had to pay for both train tickets. It's an awful lot cheaper travelling round Britain by yacht than it is by saver return.

We left the marina in Lowestoft for the early bridge opening at 7, motoring in a flat calm back past the rotting hulks and out to sea. Though we saw nothing more than a force 3, it was northerly, so again we motorsailed into the wind. The last few days had seen strong northerlies, so the main was useful in damping down the rolling in the swell. We saw one other sail on the same course as we rode the ebb tide inshore of the large windfarm off the coast. Rounding the north hump of East Anglia we set a course of 324 magnetic and stayed on that course for nearly 200 uneventful miles.

> *Pondering... Whilst at home I had bought a new tillerpilot and it was a revelation. You just needed to point the boat on a course then press a single button and the tillerpilot would keep her on that course for ever! If you wanted to change course you could do so at an accuracy of a single degree at a time if you wanted! This was such a total revelation compared to the old, crap, broken tillerpilot that I felt rather foolish for not having replaced it before. I resisted the temptation to chuck the old one in the sea.*

Zophiel is a mere dot, crossing the border

Our course of 324 magnetic took us just outside the Dudgeon Shoal cardinal buoy and dodged a number of gas platforms that evening. As night fell it was with a bit of trepidation that I left Anna to her watch. This being her first substantial night sail I wasn't sure how she would take to sailing through the pitch dark, alone and out of sight of land. In fact she really enjoyed the experience. During the night the 324 course avoided the shipping going in and out of the Humber, just missed the point of Flamborough head by about a mile and fetched us up just outside Whitby harbour at ten a.m. It was nice to get back into a rhythm of watches and just keep going through the night. Most of this summer's cruise has involved solo dashes from one port to another in a single day. The mindset changes completely when you go beyond a day sail and get into a watch keeping system, and after a while the miles pass much more quickly as well.

After 150 miles it had been our intention to go into Whitby and spend the night there before pressing on. It's reputed to be a nice place and the pilot book, with its gushing language and hyperbole, was fulsome in its praise. Arriving at ten a.m. in perfect, if calm, conditions, it seemed rather daft to stop, so we carried on towards

Blyth, setting a course, of course, of 324 magnetic.

The day was as cloudless and fine as the previous one as we passed the ports of the Tees, the Wear and the Tyne and entered the Royal Northumberland Yacht Club at Blyth that evening. Just over 200 miles in two days and a night. The members of RNYC were competing to reinforce their image as a friendly club and it was difficult to find space to jump ashore amongst all the volunteers who rushed to take our lines. They were very chatty and interested in our trip, offered us lifts and – crucially – accepted Scottish money in the clubhouse bar aboard an old light ship, where we had a good value hearty meal.

> *Pondering...* *Outside the immediate environs of the club the dockside at Blyth is extraordinarily run down and knackered. Whilst elsewhere in Europe they would have responded to the demise of the commercial port and the demand for leisure services by redeveloping the docks, the British planning system - with its strict and repressive zoning – and the British attitude to boats and the sea – have led to the erection of unscaleable grey fences all around the dock area. Instead of trying to improve this wasteland it has been fenced off. The rows of local houses just face a row of twenty foot high grey fence with razor wire. It is unclear what this fence is protecting. Perhaps the authorities fear that the people of Blyth will make off with some rusty corrugated iron or a pile of rubble. Again putting myself in the position of a visiting Dutch yachtsman the feeling would be one of disbelief that such a rich economy, with an evident demand for the leisure use of the sea, could countenance such ghettoisation and create such a wasteland.*

> *...and more Pondering...* *The pilot book waxes lyrical about the happy coexistence of yachting, fishing and commerce at Blyth and, seeing a big sign at the other side of the harbour saying 'FUEL', I enquired at the yacht club when the fuelling facility was open. They explained that the bloke who runs the diesel pump refuses to sell fuel to yachts, because it's not worth his while turning out. I asked whether he would sell fuel to lots of yachts at the same time. I said that I could take 100 litres and that I wouldn't mind paying more per litre as a premium for (relatively) small amounts. They shrugged their shoulders. It is impossible to get fuel in Blyth. You must motor the 3 hour return trip to the Tyne or waste a day getting into Amble, accessible only at high tide, or bring it in cans. So much for happy coexistence. The bloke fuelling fishing boats would rather simply refuse to accept cash than fuel the hundreds of yachts which pass through.*

Again we had to leave Zoph for the week, so when I came back the following week it was with a 25 litre can of diesel from Port Edgar, cunningly disguised as a rucksack. At last we had a south westerly forecast. The wind had been northerly, so I motorsailed off into a five foot swell from the north east. The wind increased and soon I was under full sail on a beam reach in up to 25 knots apparent. The breeze was fluky however and for the first 3 hours I turned the engine on and off 6 or 7 times. Anna had come for the weekend but elected not to sail. So she did vicarious sailing, following me by car along the coast and stopping off at old lady tea rooms along the way. Though fluky the wind generally increased and at times I was doing nearly 8 knots over the bottom with the tide. Aside from some creel boats there were few boats, though it was nice to see that most of the lobster pot boats were still traditional Northumberland cobles.

Passing the entrance to Lindisfarne I saw a large Jeanneau under main only, presumably waiting for the tide to go in and anchor off Holy Island. For a moment I wondered if she might be Erin, last seen heading across the line at the start of the North Sea race, which she won, Then I realised she couldn't be, since she had a reef in the main in a force 3 and on the foredeck was a crappy old Avon Redcrest dinghy, with the familiar yellow stripe. I was certain that Erin would have a more state-of-the-art tender than this. Anyway they waved cheerily and I waved back.

For the last couple of hours the wind rose to a force five or six and I'd have considered a reef but for the fact that the sea was smooth and I didn't have far to go. I had an exhilarating sail past Berwick on Tweed. The Berwick on Tweed lifeboat came zooming out and approached Zoph. Someone on the foredeck shouted over to ask whether it was OK to contact us by radio. This seemed an odd course of action which didn't take full advantage of the radio medium, but I assented. They had me count slowly from 1 to 10 for them over the radio, so that they could set something or other. Very odd, but doubtless necessary.

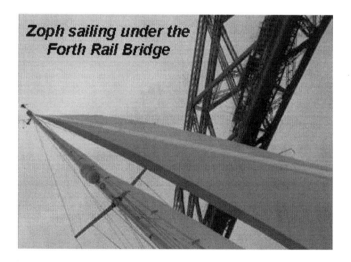

Zoph sailing under the Forth Rail Bridge

Part 10 – Home Sweet Home

I arrived in Eyemouth with the wind still increasing and as another Port Edgar yacht, the small bilge keeled Westerly 'Therapy' was heading out northwards in the increasingly strong wind. I met Anna on the long pontoon in the harbour. Eyemouth is a pretty town with a whole pile of pubs. It has to be said that the inside of a lot of the pubs doesn't live up to their apparent appeal from a distance, but we found one place which looked good for a meal, albeit a bit yoof oriented and dominated by brands of lager competing with one another for how cold they could be.

> **Pondering...** *Outside this pub was a long review of the restaurant which didn't inspire confidence. It featured a picture of yet another Port Edgar boat, 'Bluestreak' and was a section nicked from the blog of her skipper, Charlie Hussey', about a cruise to Eyemouth, in which he said that the bar looked pretty good and the food might be OK but everyone was too pissed to bother eating. You'd have thought even a lukewarm review from the Berwick Bugle would inspire more confidence. Charlie's review was however reasonably accurate and I can now add that the food was OK and the service friendly and efficient.*

After a meal and a couple of pints we headed back to Zoph, to find Erin, of course, tied up behind us on the pontoon. We were invited on board for a beer by Cap'n Erin and Cap'n 'Kermit', yet another Port Edgar boat and were soon joined by the rest of the crew, who wanted to know why I hadn't been more effusively friendly when I passed them off Lindisfarne. Sorry. The last time we'd sat aboard Erin was nearly 3 months before in Norway and seeing her again did feel like something of a home coming.

I wondered at the strength of the beer as soon the glasses started sliding all over the table and I felt decidedly unstable. Of course Erin's deep keel was sitting on the bottom as the spring tide went out. As luck would have it she leaned away from the pontoon instead of towards it and pretty soon there was a yawning gulf and a five foot drop down to the pontoon as Erin heeled over at about 15 degrees. The skipper managed either to affect a total confidence and lack of concern at this turn of events, or he genuinely wasn't worried, which seems unlikely. After a quick course in mountaineering we managed to abseil onto the pontoon and went back to Zoph, who was still afloat with her shallower draft.

The forecasts were incredibly mixed and incompatible in the morning, but the inshore waters, just barely picked up on our dodgy VHF, had westerlies of force 5 to 7 and possibly 8. Though we weren't convinced that this was actually what would happen, it didn't seem unreasonable to decide to stay in port rather than heading off solo with a gale on the nose forecast, so once again we left Zoph for the week, driving back to Edinburgh through unremitting driving rain. Later the crew of Erin said that it hadn't been that bad, but who needs the hassle of sailing 50 miles westwards constantly expecting a westerly gale .

The next weekend I went back to Eyemouth by train and bus for one last passage. In the morning I began motorsailing in a flat calm, but the wind soon got up to 25 knots just behind the port beam, then moderated to 15 to 25 knots on a fine reach. It was good sailing past Dunbar. Once you can see the Bass Rock from the south you're looking at the same stuff you can see from near Port Edgar and it feels like you've nearly arrived. I hardened up past the Bass Rock, then Craigleith and Fidra, from where I could see the Forth rail and road bridges for the first time in over 3 months. A real sign of approaching home.

I risked upsetting half of Europe by raising the Stan's flag, the red ensign and the courtesy flags of everywhere we'd visited from the starboard spreaders. All very improper and an indulgence, but what the hell. After a while I was plugging against the tide, albeit it was neaps, so put the engine on for a bit. I hardly ever motor when sailing locally on the Forth so I turned the engine off and we beat in past the Oxcars lighthouse under full sail in company with a couple of Port Ed boats with reefed mains.

At 5.45 pm I passed under the bridges and tied up on one of the many vacant pontoon berths at Port Ed, helped by a reception committee of Anna, her sister Elena and Ian Cameron.

Postscript

> **Pondering...** *The following day there was a message left on our answer machine at home... "Hello, this is Port Edgar Marina. We've found your boat on one of our pontoons. What's it doing there? You can't just come here and moor you know. Don't you know there's a waiting list?!". It's just their way of saying 'welcome home'. The marina staff often seem to misinterpret the term 'waiting list'. Port Edgar is more than half empty over the winter months, but because they make a list of boats and you have to wait for them to decide which berth you are on, they say there is a 'waiting list'. You have to know the code to interpret what they are saying.*

I was glad to get home after what had been a very enjoyable, but long and often exhausting trip. A round trip of 2215 miles through 9 countries (if you count England and Scotland as two), almost exactly half of which was sailed single handed. Rather more than half was done under engine or at least with a bit of assistance from the motor, which is always a disappointing aspect of cruising, but still a reasonable distance for a 27ft plastic bucket.

A North Sea circuit including the Skaggerak, Kattegat and a tiny corner of the Baltic and back is no Spitsbergen or Atlantic circuit, but I was quite chuffed. Though I'd carefully avoided the really bad conditions we had that summer, we had been out in gale force winds on a number of occasions and seen major thunderstorms and eight foot seas pushing us onto a lee shore. But by far the worst, most unpleasant, wet and choppy conditions, with standing waves that stopped us dead, were not on the second cruise but the first one – trying to get out through the Forth rail bridge on that first morning. The only incidence of seasickness all summer was while we were sitting on a mooring at Aberdour, four miles from home on the Forth.

On the first day back working I thought that I definitely needed a good long time away from thoughts of boats and the sea. Perhaps a month or so without sailing or making any more plans. Zoph was looking a bit the worse for wear and I had a list of jobs to do as long as the mast, off of which, for example, the VHF aerial had fallen about 1500 miles ago. But I could leave all that for a while. There's plenty of other stuff I've got to do after all. I'll just knuckle down and get on with work and stuff. Yes, definitely a month or so with no thoughts of sailing.

A few hours later Anna came home from work. "So, um, I thought I'd perhaps go for a sail on Saturday and, by the way, how do you fancy the Lofoten Islands next year?" I said.

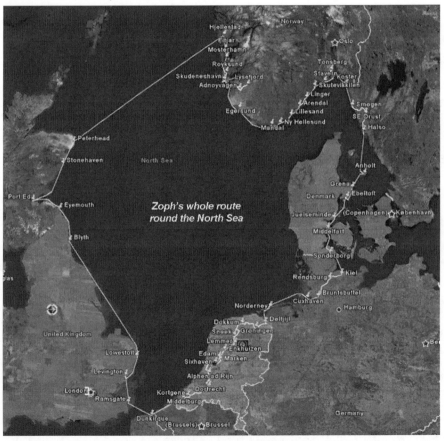

The Beginning

This is one of four books so far describing Zophiel's cruises.

*"**Skagerrak and Back:** Zophiel's Two Summer Cruises in 2007"* is the first one and is a relatively short account of a North Sea circuit.

*"**Floating Low to Lofoten**"* describes her trip from Edinburgh north to the Norwegian arctic and back in 2008.

*"**A Gigantic Whinge on the Celtic Fringe:** A Total and Complete Circumnavigation of Ireland and Britain by the Slightly Truncated Irish Route"* is, if you can get past the misleading title, just about a trip around Ireland in 2011.

*"**Bobbing to the Baltic**"* is the tale of her 2012 trip along much the same route as described in Griff Rhys Jones' book 'To the Baltic with Bob', but with a pile more photos and descriptions of a lot more good places to stop.

I have also written two books about my travels – without Zophiel – in parts of Asia, Africa and Central America little frequented by Europeans. They are entitled *"Travels with my Rant"* and *"The Front of Beyond"*.

There's more sailing tales at **http://www.edge.me.uk/Sailinghome.htm**, where you will also find the colour photos contained in these volumes.

Printed in Great Britain
by Amazon.co.uk, Ltd.,
Marston Gate.